HAUNTED TOLEDO

CHRIS BORES

Published by Haunted America
A Divison of The History Press
Charleston, SC
www.historypress.com

Front cover: The Oliver House.

First published 2022

Manufactured in the United States

ISBN 9781467150835

Library of Congress Control Number: 2022937928

CONTENTS

PREFACE

I f you live in Toledo and have a fascination with ghosts, hauntings and the paranormal, this city has a lot to offer. When I started compiling information for this book, I loved finding out that many places I visited in the past were actually haunted. I discovered so many that I had to limit myself to just covering buildings within the city limits of Toledo. I made one or two exceptions, but when it came to Maumee and Sylvania locations like Fort Meigs, Old Governor's Inn, Levi and Lilacs and the Wolcott House, they had to be set aside for this rodeo. Even without those additions, I hope you'll find that this book is still quite the beast of comprehensive haunted hot spots in Toledo.

For those of you who don't know me, my name is Chris Bores. I have been exploring Toledo's most haunted locations for over a decade now. I was a ghost tour guide at the Collingwood Arts Center for five years and have conducted tours at Oliver House, been let into sensitive locations like the Toledo Airport, been on all the local news stations, been a guest on national radio shows and even filmed a segment for truTV's *Hardcore Pawn* to spread my knowledge and love of the paranormal. I am so glad The History Press sought me out for this project because I had much to interject. In fact, I was dumbfounded how a book like this had never been written before. The only books that even dive into Toledo's haunted past are Chris Woodyard's Haunted Ohio six-volume book series. Unfortunately, her information was outdated, and she only visited two locations: the Collingwood Arts Center and Timko's Soup and Such (now El Camino's), which many don't remember, since the place went out of business during the '80s.

Within these pages, I tried very hard to peel back as many layers of history that each location gave up. I dug through so many library archives that my head was spinning by the end of each research day. I wanted to appeal to not only ghost enthusiasts but history buffs as well. I really went above and beyond in trying to figure out what happened in these locations— who died where and why. In fact, I spent so much time researching all the biggest tragedies in Toledo, I swear I should've titled this book *Toledo's Most Gruesome Deaths*.

In *Haunted Toledo*, you'll find fifty locations that I painfully researched by leaving no stone unturned. The history I bring to light is pretty amazing, and I'm sure most of what I cover is considered lost history in many circles. For instance, did you know the Toledo Zoo was only started because it was part of an amusement park? Did you know that the Toledo Yacht Club was built at Point Place because they had a Cedar Point–type amusement park right down the street from it? Did you know the Franklin Park Mall area once contained a funeral home that now causes paranormal activity to occur? Or how about the explosion that blew up a whole city block near the Commodore Perry Hotel? I even dug into the urban legend of Chalky and found out its lost origin story! I swear the process of gathering information for this book must've been channeled by the restless spirits themselves hoping for peace in the afterlife, because facts came to me very serendipitously.

Chris Bores investigating the Gerber House at the Collingwood Arts Center. *Chris Bores.*

Rolling back the history on all these locations was a monumental task, but I feel the end result was worth it. I even sought help from many Toledo historical groups. I kept beating the bushes for so many personal ghost stories, I'm sure I was on the verge of being kicked out! I'd like to give a special thanks to all of them for putting up with me. My goal was to make this book a group effort from the community. I wanted to include as many stories and quotes as I could and give credit where it was due. There are a lot of great local ghost hunting groups around town, and I tried to mention each one where it made sense. Without the community helping me, this book would not have been possible.

If you decide to check out any of these locations for yourself, please be respectful of the area and the people working there. I'm sure this book will be used as a reference guide for decades to come, so remember, just like people, ghosts can also come and go as they wish. A place haunted today might not be haunted tomorrow.

Chris Bores's Classifications of Ghosts

I've been at this ghost hunting thing for over a decade now, and I've come up with a handy classification system when it comes to ghosts. This is something that helps me figure out why ghosts do what they do, what they need and how to help them. So, the following are a few classifications I reference throughout this book.

Now, tuck yourself in, sit back and turn down the lights. Things are about to get creepier in Toledo as we pull back the curtain. I will be your tour guide through the afterlife as we begin our adventures through *Haunted Toledo*.

Hungry Ghosts

The term *hungry* is derived from the *Tibetan Book of the Dead*'s concept of a hungry ghost. They are dubbed "hungry" because they have a psychological hunger that causes them to cling or crave things like unfinished business, attachments to items, goals, people or even human forms.

Parasitical Ghosts

These spirits experience an extreme level of craving and hunger to the point of addiction. They constantly feed off locations, emotions and people.

Confused Ghosts

These spirits are locked in state of confusion that limits them from knowing basic things like if they are dead, who they are, where they are and more. This confusion stems from a denial of death, the way they died or an extreme level of hunger. This eventually leads to all sorts of problems that trap them inside of a world of illusion created by their own mind.

Wandering Ghosts

These spirits have no affiliation with the locations they haunt. They enter one area from another because they are either passing by or have been attracted into it. They know they are dead, have extroverted personalities and can be considered tourists of the afterlife.

Stuck Ghosts

These spirits remain in a location because they either feel emotionally stuck to it or are physically bound to it through a ritual or act. They are mostly introverted personality types that know they are dead but are working through it.

Destructive Ghosts

These spirits have mindsets that have spun out of control. They lash out at others and love to spread misery, disorder and destruction. Their emotions are wild with anger and are comparable to a child throwing a temper tantrum. They can be dangerous to deal with since they can manipulate the physical world as they see fit.

1
OLIVER HOUSE

The Oliver House at 27 Broadway Street is probably the most notorious haunted location in Toledo. When I first moved here and told people that I hunt ghosts, Oliver House was the one place they always brought up. Its ghostly reputation is known to all. What made this building even more of a golden goose was that the owners wouldn't allow any ghost hunters in to properly ghost hunt it. They were very protective of their ghosts. After ten years of dreaming of my chance to investigate the Oliver House, fate intervened, and the owners allowed me exclusive access to their facility. My time there did not disappoint, and it definitely lived up to its reputation.

This historic building was named after Major William Oliver from Cincinnati. He fought in the Battle of 1812 and was one of the original settlers of Toledo. He was determined to make his mark on the community, so he built the first high-class hotel in town. He picked Broadway Street because the train depot was located there. He wanted his hotel to be the first thing anyone saw as they entered the city. The building took seven years to complete, and sadly, Mr. Oliver died before the hotel was finished. His daughter Hattie and son-in-law James Hall took over operations and had their grand opening celebration on July 1, 1859.

At the time, Toledo was still a relatively small city. It had only been founded twenty-six years prior, in 1833. It had seen little growth because Michigan had been fighting over the Toledo Territory until 1837. Once that was dealt with, the city built the Miami and Erie Canal in 1845, which provided water to everyone in town. This set the stage for the Oliver House to open in 1859.

Oliver House, 1880s. *Toledo Public Library.*

The swanky hotel offered many enticing amenities to wealthy businessmen visiting Toledo. Each of the 171 rooms had running water, limited indoor plumbing, fireplaces, private rooms and steam heaters. The hotel was also the first to introduce wallpaper and gaslights to the city. The staff even had to post signs around the hotel advising guests not to blow the gaslight flames out or else they would be dead in the morning from the fumes.

As one walked into the front entrance, the check-in desk greeted you, along with a large table full of daily newspapers. The stairs on the right lead to the second floor, which contained a bar, a billiard room (also used as the men's smoking lounge) and a barbershop. The stairs to the left lead to offices, hotel rooms and a dining room that could also be converted into a ballroom. Out back were the icehouse, coal storage and horse stables. Rooms started at $2.50 a night, while the hotel staff only made $0.10 a day. It's rumored that President Abraham Lincoln once stayed overnight while attending a friend's funeral, but it's confirmed that President Ulysses S. Grant visited in 1873 with General William Sherman.

After a great run, Oliver's daughter sold the building in 1884 to Frank Oakes and Henry Millar. Unfortunately, the hotel's competition was becoming fierce, since traveling businessmen preferred staying at hotels downtown like the American Hotel (1868), the Boody House Hotel (1870)

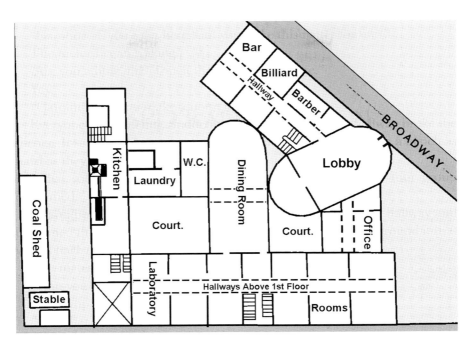

The original 1888 Oliver House floor plan. *Chris Bores.*

In the 1930s, the main lobby was partitioned off for use by individual vendors. *Toledo Public Library.*

and the Monticello Hotel (1891). In order to keep the Oliver House profitable, half the building was rented out for warehouse space in 1895 to companies like Berdan and Co. By 1900, the other half of the building was slowly turning into a boardinghouse for the poor. Then in 1919, the floundering business was purchased by Riddle Lighting Company. It gutted the entire building and sold off all the marble fireplaces, mahogany paneling and the ballroom accents. It installed an elevator near the original grand staircase, then sectioned off the main lobby into individual retail spaces that venders could rent out. One of those venders was the Ohio Savings Bank, which installed two large bank vaults in the back of the room. Once the Great Depression of the 1930s hit Toledo, the Oliver House became a flophouse for the poor.

The building limped along into the 1990s until Jim and Patricia Appold purchased the Oliver House and restored it as best as they could to its former glory while adding in restaurants, pubs, meeting rooms and apartments into its floor plan. As the remodel began, workers slowly began noticing the odd ghostly activity occurring around them. It was as if they had just awoken the dead.

Cheryl King recalled, "I worked there when it was the Oliver House Development Corporation, and I worked late nights. That place is very haunted. I saw and heard things that could not be explained. I was working one night, had to go to the bathroom and walked by what used to be the grand ballroom. There were several shadow figures, and it was really spooky looking. We also heard moaning and loud noises coming from the basement. Someone said there was a tunnel underneath."

OLIVER HOUSE GHOSTS

For years, the Oliver House staff has had front-row seats to all the paranormal activity taking place in the building. According to former waitress Krystal Smith, "That place is crazy haunted! I didn't see anything, but I felt it! I'd walk to Rockwell's when it was closed, and my hair would stand up. I felt like I wasn't welcome. Many times, it was terrifying."

Employee Shelly Smart added, "I saw a ghost up on the top floor. It scared the crap out of me!"

Anna Boo-kowski also shared, "I used to work at the Oliver House for three years, and I've had several paranormal experiences, like things falling even though nobody was around. One time, a bartender was filling up a growler of beer and it flew across the bar and shattered. When I would close late by myself, I would sometimes hear my name being whispered. I've seen a black figure in the basement, and I've had a little girl follow me around." Even in the daytime, Anna experienced activity. "When I opened in the morning by myself, I would feel a strong presence of someone else around me."

The current staff told me they've also experienced things, like dinner plates moving or falling over without explanation. Not only do the workers experience activity, but the costumers do as well. Tina Hand Mutscheller remembered, "The first time we ate there was for a dinner with my husband's clients. I commented on the tablecloth moving just by my leg. My husband said, 'It must be a vent blowing.' I went with that theory until the tablecloth flipped up as if someone were holding it out! I jumped up and made him switch seats with me. The waitress came back, and I told her what happened. She said, 'Yeah, this place is haunted!'"

Thankfully, after hearing all these stories and combining them with my own personal encounters, I've been able come up with a list of over ten spirits that haunt the building.

Ghost Children

Ghost children are found just about everywhere in the main sections of the building. They love to play and tug at peoples' clothing, poke customers, move things around and even pinch a butt cheek on occasion. They basically feel like the building is their playground and can usually be seen by other kids visiting the Oliver House.

In the main banquet room, there are three ghost children that haunt the area; two young boys and a blond-haired girl. The girl is usually seen in the doorway of the steps leading down to the ground-level hallway. Rumor has it that she loves puppies, since she has been known to appear if someone brings one in. It's rumored that the little girl comes from the flophouse days.

As for the two ghost boys, it's said by medium Sirena La Point that she feels they both have strong ties to a local banking company and come from a rich family with a nanny that takes care of them. This is pretty amazing, since I ran across a newspaper article dated December 16, 1859, that supports these claims. It reported that a seven-year-old boy named Clarence Clark was the son of bank owner W. Clark of the Exchange Bank. Unfortunately, Clarence was playing around on the grand stairway banister just off the main lobby area (around where the elevator is now), and as he tried sliding down the railing, he lost his grip and fell twenty-five feet to the hallway below. The impact crushed his skull, causing him to bleed out and die within two hours.

There are a few other ghost children in the Oliver House, and you'll find them in Rockwell's third-floor Fireside Room. Whenever I've encountered any of the ghost children, my interactions have always been very short and brief. They seem very playful, with short attention spans. Every time I bring in a new ghost gadget in for them to play with, they are interested in it briefly before growing tired of it and moving on. As parents know, that is pretty typical of most children that age.

Murdered Maid

When the Oliver House was a high-class hotel, the staff was comprised of many Black waiters, maids and housekeepers. There is a story that one of the maids wanted to make more money on the side, so she prostituted herself out to the wealthy men staying at the hotel. After getting involved with one repeat customer, the man grew concerned about his reputation being tarnished and hired two men to kidnap the girl and kill her. After doing so, they wrapped her body up in a carpet, snuck it out through a series of cargo tunnels underneath the hotel and dumped it into the Maumee River. It's said that to this day, the maid haunts the hotel because she wants people to know what really happened to her.

One medium who visited the Oliver House sensed the maid's energy right away. According to B. Bailey, "My wife is psychic and says there is a woman at the brewery. She has been there since the place was a hotel. She was murdered and doesn't understand."

As for myself, I've always made contact with the maid in the banquet room. She mostly likes to interact with my Ovilus ghost hunting device. This is a tool I call a voice box for the dead, since it takes the energy in an area and associates words to it. The first time I interacted with her, the Ovilus picked up two words in succession: *highway* and *malicious*. This was amazing, since using both words together helps paint a story of how she was killed in a *malicious* way and then reveals how she was taken out of the hotel through a *highway* of tunnels.

It's also amazing because every time I have used the Ovilus in the banquet room, I always get the word *highway* to appear. This even happened in front of the local Channel 13 news cameras when they came out to do a story at the Oliver House in 2021. Not only did the word appear once after turning the device on, but it also happened again ten minutes later.

Billiard Room Man

When it comes to the former billiard room on the second floor, people have reported hearing a man's voice haunting this location. Others have heard unexplainable footsteps, soft talking and murmurs and doors closing shut. A few EVPs of this male have also been recorded in the room.

When I was trying to figure out who this mystery man is, I was able to compile quite the list. Lawyer George Baxter died by suicide at the Oliver House in 1865, State Senator James Hall died in his room in 1868, New Mexico's ex-governor John Greiner died of paralysis here in 1871, Willis Chapell died by suicide from morphine overdose in 1889 and an unnamed man fell out a fourth-floor window to his death in 1916.

Crying Teenager

Nestled in the hallway between the banquet hall and Rockwell's restaurant is a set of bathrooms. A few employees have heard unexplained sounds of a girl sobbing when no one is around at night. It's said these phantom sounds date to when a ballroom dance was held at the hotel in the late 1800s. The story involves a teenage girl from the upper class falling in love with a boy from the lower class, and they would meet there every weekend. After her mother found out, she confronted the daughter in the women's restroom. She was furious and forbid her daughter from seeing the boy again. She then ripped a pearl necklace off her daughter's neck that she wore for the boy. It's said that this painful memory is scarred into this area.

Military Wife

Rockwell's Fireside Room is where you'll find the ghost of the military wife. This female spirit is one of my favorites to interact with, since she is pretty feisty. On April 29, 1898, her husband, along with 846 other Toledo military troops, was called to fight in the Spanish-American War. Everyone gathered at the Oliver House for one last drink before the men departed the city by train. Shortly after her husband left, the woman found out she was pregnant. Then the war ended two weeks later, and all the soldiers came back home, except three. One of them was the wife's husband. Was he killed in action? Did he skip town?

Well, this is where things get a little murky. According to medium Sirena La Point, she feels that the husband didn't return home because he left his wife for another woman. Unfortunately, I've come to a different conclusion based on my own personal interactions with the wife. During my investigation, the wife made it very clear that her husband died on the battlefield and that she received a letter in the mail about it. This account would also fit the historical record, since it's documented that all three men who didn't return died from fatal wounds on the battlefield.

But whatever the real story may be, the wife was devastated by her husband's death, and her emotions caused her to miscarry and lose the baby. Since her husband was also the breadwinner of the family, she became very poor. When the building became a boardinghouse in the 1900s, the woman moved in and lived out the remainder of her life there. She took it upon herself to watch over the many children who also lived there, and she became their teacher and educated them. She has a great love for the children, and it's said that if you try interacting with them, she'll step in to prevent it.

Any pregnant woman who wants to visit the Fireside Room will often feel light touching sensations on their arms or a light pushing or pulling sensation around their feet. This is because the military wife is trying to assist these pregnant ladies with walking so they don't trip over.

R.J. Nowotka was lucky enough to catch a rare glimpse of the military wife one evening while visiting the brewery. "I went up in Rockwell's when it was closed to check out the old cash register they had up there. As we were leaving, we saw a lady in white staring out the window! I looked back up, and she was gone."

Bashful Child

There is one ghost child in the Rockwell's area that I have labeled the bashful child. I call her that because she follows people around and will run off if you try interacting with her.

Medium Sirena La Point has spent years trying to unlock her backstory. During most of her encounters with the young girl, La Point would see the little girl approach her and say, "My dad, my dad!" then disappear. This went on for years until one day, she saw the little girl in Rockwell's and pointed out the window. As La Point looked outside, she saw the mental image of the train station that used to be there during the early 1900s. She then saw two thugs beat up a man. "My dad," the little girl cried again. After revealing this painful scene to La Point, the little girl vanished, and her spirit hasn't been seen since.

For weeks after I heard this story, I couldn't stop thinking about it. It broke my heart thinking she was still reliving the pain of seeing her dad getting beat up and killed over and over again after one hundred years or so. Thankfully, my research led me to an article dated July 25, 1878, that helped shed light on this whole ordeal. This article reported that Hamlin Huber was robbed by two thugs in front of the train depot and was beaten within an inch of his life. The newspaper also pointed out that he was a father. Wow—this was exactly what La Point saw. There was only one little fact that was off. It turns out that the man had a son, not a daughter. So, either the newspaper reporter got this small detail wrong, or perhaps the man was the father of two children and the newspaper only reported on the son because his daughter was upstairs watching her dad get beaten up. Unfortunately, this may be a riddle I'll never be able to solve, but the newspaper was so accurate that I'm fairly confident Hamlin Huber was the man La Point saw in her vision. I'm just glad I can sleep easy knowing that this little girl isn't haunting the building because she saw her father die in front of her that day.

Indians and Captains

The most popular online rumor surrounding the Oliver House is that it's haunted by a Native or a former Navy captain. Unfortunately, when it comes to the Native, I believe that rumor was started back in the 1990s, when the owners dug up the back parking lot and discovered a body around the top step of the Maumee Brewing Company entrance. In order to appease the body's spirit, a Native shaman was called in to bless it and rebury it. According to previous manager Neal Kovacik, "We had a tribe from out west come out and perform a ceremony to rebury the remains. Seeing that an Indian shaman blessed the area, the story might've gotten mixed up that an Indian haunts the land."

When it comes to the captain, the rumor states that a previous captain from the 1800s still haunts the building. This might be a case in which a story spawned out of the billiard room ghost because I haven't found any evidence to support this spirit's existence either.

Mobsters

It's well documented that a few bars and establishments in downtown Toledo had ties to the mob in the early 1900s. It's said that the back half of the downstairs basement was used to make beer for smuggling around town. A few spiritual mediums have also picked up on a dark energy in the area that tells them to back off and stay out. It's speculated that these basement rooms were used by the mob to "wack" their enemies. One stroll through this area late at night, and you'll get uneasy feelings of something not being right.

Romantic Couple

In the Maumee Brewing restaurant, there have been sightings of a pair of romantic ghosts out on a date. According to local astrologer Janet Amid, "I was having dinner with my friend in the casual restaurant. I saw a man and woman walk in with a 1940s look. His hair was slicked back with a bowtie. The woman had blond hair with her old-style dress. I thought they were part of a costume party. I said, 'Look how strange they look,' and pointed at them. My friend couldn't see them. They then faded out." As soon as they did, her friend finally caught a glimpse of them out of the corner of his eye and exclaimed, "What the hell was that?"

MY GHOST INVESTIGATIONS

When I finally got my chance to investigate the Oliver House, I was shocked at how many spirits I was able to interact with. The first ghost I encountered was the spirit of the young boy in the banquet room. This spirit was very playful and refused to give me any hits on the meter (called meter spikes) on command. The boy was having more fun spiking the meter whenever I least expected it. Every time I began talking to the camera and stopped paying attention to the meter, the thing would go off by blinking. That happened three times in a row.

Later, while trying to figure out the boy's name, I used a Panasonic RR-DR60 digital recorder in the hopes of recording the answer. The device's low recording sampling rate helps pick up noises and voices that shouldn't be there. After asking a few questions with the audio recorder, I picked out this set of responses.

"What is your name?"

"Mike."

"Are you playing with our devices?"

"No."

Since there are two ghost boys reported to be in this area, I am led to believe that this boy's name is Clarence, while the other is Michael.

Another sensitive location I was granted access to was the infamous underground tunnels. To my knowledge, no other person has ever explored this area aside from upper-level management. As I made my way inside, I felt the air become thick. A few hundred years ago, the body of the murdered maid was said to have passed through here on the way to the river. I placed my EDI meter on the ground and decided to ask about the murder. It took a few minutes to get a response, but the spiking pattern was pretty revealing. "Did anyone pass through here on the way out?"

My voice was interrupted by lights appearing on the meter.

I asked a few more questions. Nothing happened. Then I asked, "Were you brought through this way on the way out to the—"

Another spike. Yes.

"So, were you brought through here on the way out to the Toledo Bay?"

The meter spiked a third time. Yes.

At this point, the meter spiking pattern was very obvious as to what was being conveyed, since the spirit only lit up the device when I got to the part in my question about passing through that area. I asked a few more questions, but the ghost was tight-lipped after that. It seems this spirit does not want to reveal any more about this event.

MILITARY WIFE ENCOUNTER

As I made my way to Rockwell's Fireside Room, I really felt like I needed to explore the military wife's backstory by making contact with her. At the time, I was told her husband left for the war and never came back because he ran off with another woman. I wanted to verify that story. I pulled out my Ovilus (otherwise known as a voice box for the dead, as it associates words to certain energies it picks up) and placed a REM pod on a nearby table. This nifty gadget has all kinds of alarms and lights that go off when a ghost triggers it. As I coaxed the spirit out with some comforting words, my voice was drowned out by the REM pod chirping to life.

"Great! Can you back away from that please?"

The pod instantly fell silent.

"Can you touch that again?"

A split second later, the Ovilus went off.

"Pluto," it said.

"Pluto?" My mind instantly went to the image of Mickey Mouse's dog companion. Since the building was used as a flophouse in the 1930s, the children at the time could have been aware of him. "You mean the dog Pluto?"

The Ovilus spit out two more words: *eat* and *sent*.

"I gotta know who's telling me these words. Is it the wife?"

The REM pod went off again. Yes.

"What did you mean by the word *sent*? It reminds me of your husband that was sent off to the war."

My train of thought was derailed by another REM pod spike. Yes.

"Am I right?"

The pod kept spiking. Yes.

I pulled out my Panasonic recorder again to see if I could record any responses. I asked a series of hard questions. "Are you sad?"

"Get out!" was her response in the form of an EVP. It was done in a hushed toned whisper.

"Are you mad because the children might've talked to me on this device and said Pluto? Did you get angry about that? I know you're very territorial of these kids—"

"F———!" she exclaimed.

Whoa—I did not expect to be cussed out. I had obviously struck a nerve. I couldn't back down now. I had to dig deeper. "I notice every time I say the word *sent*, you hit that device. Is that a trigger word for you? Are you still trying to work through that pain?"

No response.

I then pulled out a newer gadget called a Paranormal Puck. This little round electronic device acts with the same technology as Ovilus, but you

Chris Bores investigating the Rockwell's Fireside Room and interacting with the military wife with an Ovilus ghost hunting device. *Chris Bores.*

can input questions through an app and get answers. I've seen this device in action, and it can pull up the same words from a spirit that a spiritual medium can, so there seems to be some validity to it.

"What is your name?" I typed into the Paranormal Puck app.

Tom.

"Are you teaching the children?"

French.

"Are you still recovering from your husband leaving?

Killed.

"Killed?" I restated. Could the story of the husband leaving his wife for another woman be wrong? Was the real story that he never came back because he was killed in action? I needed to know more.

"So, he died?" I asked.

Letter.

"Letter?" I exclaimed. "I don't know what to think of that." I said, thinking out loud. The gears inside my brain began spinning wildly like the huge engine pistons on the *Titanic*. "So, spike this REM pod if I've got that correct. Your husband's name was Tom, he was killed and you got a letter about that? Is that what happened?"

The REM pod went off again to confirm my suspicions. Yes.

I was absolutely shocked. Her answers made total sense. By giving me words like *letter*, *killed* and *sent*, I knew the emotional scarring ran deep. I spent

A mysterious greenish hued light resembling a ghost hand materializes over the REM pod device the military wife uses to interact with Chris. *Chris Bores.*

a few minutes trying to comfort her. This must have formed a bond between us, because as soon as I began talking about how ghosts can manipulate energy, she manifested right in front of me. Well, her hand did.

While watching a playback of the video on my computer, I noticed a weird light swipe across the screen right after I brought up the subject of energy manipulation. It was a green-colored light in an odd shape that resembled a human hand. I could clearly see defined fingers and a thumb. It couldn't be mistaken for anything else. The footage was shocking. At first, I thought it was a reflection of light occurring on the window behind it. The more I studied it, however, my jaw dropped, because this wasn't a reflection. The light clearly zipped over the top of the wooden frame and around the glass. If it was a reflection in the window, the light would've stopped as soon as it hit the edge. This did not.

The light also appeared for only eight frames of video, which is like appearing for one-third of a second. That is quicker than the human eye can observe. Plus, it was green in color, which also blew my mind. Any time a ghost hunter has captured a light close to this one, they have always had the night vision filter turned on. In this instance, I did not. So, this is the very first time the actual color of a ghost has been caught on film.

After the manifestation occurred, I looked at the camera and said, "I'm feeling very emotional right now." At the time, I didn't know that the light anomaly had just occurred. It was interesting to play the footage back and see that whatever she did had an impact on my emotions.

After my encounter with the spirits, I made sure to say many prayers for them so that they could heal from the scars of the past. The spirits at the Oliver House are plentiful, and if you decide to visit, be aware that almost every room has its own personal spirit haunting it.

2

COLLINGWOOD ARTS CENTER

The Collingwood Arts Center is the second most well-known haunted location in Toledo. I was proudly the first ghost tour guide of the building for almost five years, and I experienced pretty much everything the place can throw at someone. This included shadow figures and odd feelings, and I was even attacked on one occasion.

In 1872, Christian Gerber built his Gerber House at 2413 Collingwood Avenue. He was one of the wealthiest merchants in Toledo, selling grain, cutlery, hardware and spices. He spared no expense in constructing his three-story mansion that included a full basement. Gerber commissioned local Toledo architect Joseph Morehouse to design rooms with the finest wood, a lavish front-room staircase, walnut doors, marble fireplace mantles and fifteen-foot-tall ceilings. The back of the house (which no longer exists) included a kitchen, pantry and servants' quarters with a separate staircase for them to use.

Unfortunately, his budget spun out of control, and his business dried up, causing him to file for bankruptcy in the late 1890s. He was forced sell his home to wealthy Toledean George Laskey, who then turned around and sold it to the St. Ursula Academy for $25,000 in 1900. The academy quickly began constructing its campus on the land. It started by tearing down the back half of the Gerber House in 1901 to make way for a new auditorium. The structure was fireproof and built with state-of-the-art acoustics. It contained six hundred seats with four large chandeliers hanging high above. On September 5, 1905, the school's first building was completed. It turned

Mary Manse College, 1937. *Toledo Public Library.*

the Gerber House into an infirmary, while the rest of the first wing contained the auditorium, adjoining reception room, and nuns' dormitory. The second wing was used for offices, student dormitories and basement cafeteria. The third wing was used for classrooms, laboratories and even a hallway chapel.

After the school added a larger dedicated chapel room in 1918, the St. Ursula Academy sought permission from the local bishop to build a second building. He denied the request because of the cost. The St. Ursula Academy then reached out to the Mary Manse College in Bowling Green, Ohio, which said it would only finance the construction process if St. Ursula Academy merged with its institution. The St. Ursula Academy agreed to those terms, and seven more buildings were constructed over the next decade. This added more classrooms, dormitories, a gymnasium and a maintenance building to the school. The new Mary Manse College thrived for decades until the 1970s, when attendance dropped off considerably. This forced the school to file for bankruptcy in 1975 and close its doors for good in 1979.

After closing, the school sat vacant for many years. This is where things started taking a dark turn, as many squatters broke into the building and drew pentagrams all over the walls and floors for occult rituals. What better place to conjure evil than in building that was once reserved for worshipping God. A dark energy was brought into the area that would linger for years to come.

Mary Manse College, 1947. *Toledo Public Library*.

St. Ursuline's auditorium, freshly built in 1907. *St. Ursuline brochure*.

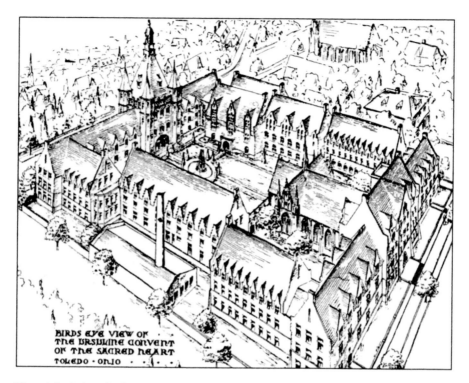

The original plans for St. Ursula Academy's campus, 1900. *Toledo Public Library*.

The cafeteria refectory located in the third-wing basement, 1907. *St. Ursuline brochure*.

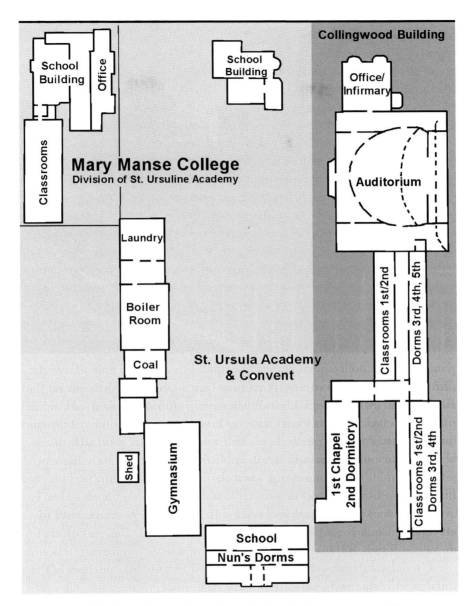

The original 1930s floor plans for Mary Manse College/St Ursula Academy. The Collingwood building grounds is shadowed darker in color on the right. *Chris Bores.*

In 1985, the abandoned school was finally purchased and became the Collingwood Arts Center. The center's goal was to provide local art students cheap and affordable dormitories. Once the rooms began filling up, the new tenants slowly realized they weren't the only ones living at the arts center.

Everyone felt a ghostly presence lurking throughout the building. Thomas Brooks said, "I spent three years as the Collingwood Arts Center director. At the time, I was a total nonbeliever in anything paranormal. After three years, I had seen enough and felt enough and am a 100-percent believer in the paranormal now."

Things got so crazy that even author Chris Woodyard caught wind of the activity taking place and did a walkthrough of the building in 1993. She documented her findings in her *Haunted Ohio* book series that helped propel the Collingwood Arts Center into local paranormal stardom. With her claims of "one spirit in the basement who wears a hateful scowl and the other upstairs who smiles and gives visitors a wave of welcome," I was curious about what I would find if I had the chance to investigate the building. Fortunately, it wouldn't take long for me to found out.

THE CHRIS BORES ERA

In 2013, I had just finished editing a paranormal documentary based on my time at the St. Augustine Lighthouse in Florida. I was looking for a haunted theater where I could show it and then conduct a ghost hunt of the building afterward. I took a meeting with the Collingwood Arts Centers management to see if I could rent out the entire facility for my paranormal needs. The lady who was running the place back then was a crotchety gray-haired woman in her seventies. She gave off the impression that she wanted to smack me for even suggesting the building could be haunted. She didn't seem thrilled at the prospect of me renting out the Collingwood for a ghost hunt, but the center was hurting for money, so management reluctantly agreed. To their surprise, the event completely sold out—they were stunned by the massive turnout.

The struggling arts center called me out of the blue a few days later and asked me to come discuss a business proposal. Management wanted to hold more ghost events with me as their ghost hunting tour guide so they could raise money for building repairs. I knew it was an opportunity of a lifetime, and I agreed very quickly. Working at the Collingwood Arts Center to hunt for ghosts was a dream come true. At the time, I was trying to hone my skills in the paranormal field, and this was the perfect playground for that. I was able to work closely with the spirits on a weekly basis and help raise money for building repairs at the same time. It was a feel-good operation that helped the center purchase a new heating system and a roof and have all the rooms repaired. No longer did the Collingwood Art Center have to rely on renting out dormitories to aging art students who were all squatters at that point, so they kicked them out. But before they did, I interviewed all of them so I could gather their paranormal stories for the first time.

HOT SPOTS

Theater

In the balcony section of the theater, it is well rumored that a nun haunts the upper-righthand side (or the house left area to be exact). A few residents who used to wander around at night saw her apparition in that location. Other people saw shadow figures in that same area.

During my tenure at the center, I wandered the balcony many countless nights during our ghost hunting events and never once saw the nun appear. I did, however, have one amazing encounter while giving a tour one evening. I set up a REM pod in the righthand balcony and was on the stage

The most popular haunting of Collingwood is the nun that haunts the theater's balcony section. I've circled the exact location where past residents have seen the ghostly nun figure appear late at night. *Toledo Public Library.*

with my tour group, telling them about the details of the haunted nun up there. I paused and looked up at the balcony and said, "If there is anyone up there, can you hit that REM pod for me?" To everyone's surprise, the pod actually went off.

"Can you do that again?" I asked.

The REM pod went off again.

"Are you the nun that haunts the balcony?"

It went off a third time. Yes.

I asked a few more questions, but nothing further occurred. What's even more shocking is that around the same moment, another ghost hunting group down in the basement of the Gerber House saw a shadow person dart across the room and peak around a pillar. I feel that whatever set off my REM pod traveled downstairs next and revealed itself to the other group.

The theater itself is also home to many odd noises and smells that materialize out of nowhere. I used to experience weird noises coming from the seating area. Stagehands always told me they would often smell the scent of coffee or toast waft in from nowhere. This is fascinating, since I was once told that the nuns always met in the theater every morning before school to have coffee and toast together. Maybe they still meet in the afterlife.

Nuns' Dormitory

Above the theater is a row of small rooms that was reserved for the nuns who lived there. Many residents witnessed shadow figures lurking around in the long hallway. I've had some interesting encounters there myself during my ghost tours. I once had a door slam shut on me while I was mid-sentence. Everyone jumped from hearing the impromptu sound.

The first time I conducted a ghost hunt in the nuns' dormitory, I was in the middle room asking for any spirit in the area to make a sound. Moments later, we heard three knocks in succession tap on the floorboards. About a month later, I was in the same room and got an amazing EVP after I asked, "Do you know what year this is?"

"Jesus," came the reply.

The voice was that of an older woman who sounded perturbed that I would ask such a ridiculous question. I assume it was one of the previous nuns.

Classroom Wing

There are many hot spot areas in the third wing of the building, with the first being the first-floor bathroom. It's said the bathroom is haunted by a teenage student named Caroline. Residents have heard her sobbing, toilets flushing and faucets turning on randomly when no one is around. The classroom right next to the bathroom is also haunted. Residents have reported hearing children's voices coming from the room late at night, while others have heard two people talking to each other. Whenever the door is opened, they find an empty room.

On the third floor, there is a room at the far end of the hallway called the Burn Room. It received that name after a fire broke out there during the late 1990s, leaving the walls badly charred for years until they were repaired in 2015. The tenant who previously lived there suffered from bad seizures, one of which claimed his life. His body sat there decomposing for a few weeks before it was discovered.

During my first ghost hunt of the building, I sat in that room with my tour group. After five minutes of sitting quietly, we all felt this darkness enter the room, causing it to become darker. It was as if any remaining light was slowly pressed out of there. It's odd to explain, but everyone could feel a shift to the room's energy. A few were freaked out by the experience. The whole ordeal lasted about a minute or so. Then the darkness slinked back from whence it came.

Fifth Floor

The fifth floor is quite the weird area to behold. One side is reserved as the theater's prop room, while the other has three small rooms next to an elevator. During the 1990s, the rooms were rented out to Mary, a retired Broadway actress. She ended up dying of old age in her room, and her body was found weeks later. I spent many nights in that area and would sometimes feel a weird heaviness in the air I couldn't explain. In August 2014, I was up there investigating and placed a K2 meter on a nearby table. I spent a half hour sitting on the floor, waiting for something to happen. It wasn't until I got up and clumsily dropped the equipment that the meter finally starting going off. It was as if the spirit was laughing at me.

"You think that's funny?" I remarked.

The meter spiked. Yes.

"Are you male?" I questioned.

No response.

"Are you female?"

No response.

"Are you neither?"

Yes.

This was an interesting answer, as sometime later, I came to the realization that some ghosts will only tell you their gender when you ask, "Were you male or female?" as opposed to "Are you male or female?"

When it comes to the prop room, I never investigated that area often because it was always locked. I was able to poke around there a couple times. When I did, I usually felt an odd energy lingering in the room. My guess was that since the room was always locked, the spirits always hid there if they wanted to get away from everyone who was investigating.

When it comes to the prop room, theater worker Thomas Brooks recalls, "A mom wanted to send her ten-year-old son up there to fetch something. When the boy came back down, he said, 'I thought all the nuns were gone from here.' The mom said, 'Yes, they moved in the '80s. Why?' The boy said, 'Because I was talking to a nun on the fifth floor who wanted to tell me how much she and the others enjoyed seeing us children practicing for our play.'"

Even one of my ghost hunting tour groups wandered up there one evening and came back down to tell me they heard a growling sound they couldn't explain.

Office Area

During the daytime hours, Pam, who works in the office, will occasionally hear voices emanating from the hallway. Another times she's witnessed a nun walking past the doorway out of the corner of her eye while she worked at her desk. She would then inspect the hallway and saw no one there.

Chapel

Reports even come from the chapel area, which is now used for the Children's Theater Workshop. Stagehands have seen shadow figures and hear noises they can't explain late at night.

Student Dormitories

I never really experienced anything in the dormitories, but I heard countless stories of how residents would be sitting in their room and see a shadow figure suddenly walk past their doorway late at night. This mostly occurred on the second floor.

A few residents even talked about a weird, dark, formless energy that would roll into their room and freak them out. One resident whom this happened to had a cat that went bonkers as the darkness crept in. My guess is that this dark thing originated from all the occult rituals performed in the basement during the 1980s.

Many residents heard unexplained footsteps coming from the floor above them. They also heard voices emanating from the hallway, where a statue of a nun holding a child is displayed. I once heard a voice coming from that area one night that I couldn't explain. After sprinting to the end of the hall, I found no one there.

Another resident told me that something on the second-floor hallway had lifted the hat off his head late one night and thrown it onto the floor. He expected to see someone behind him, but when he spun around, no one was there.

The second-level dormitory is where shadow people like roaming the halls late at night. *Chris Bores.*

Gerber House

A few residents told me they saw shadow figures around the front staircase area. I spent years investigating the Gerber House and never once encountered anything there.

Gerber House Basement

There are two basements in Collingwood. The one underneath the Gerber House is where many residents have reported seeing the most shadow person activity. They always saw them dart around pillars or disappear into walls. Since the room in the back corner is the laundry room, most of the residences would have experiences while doing their laundry. Doug Walters explained, "I was doing laundry late one night, and I saw someone against the far wall. I thought it was my friend playing a joke on me, so I called out to him, but he didn't respond. I saw him run into the corner, so I walked over there and saw it dead-ended into a solid wall. There was no one there!"

During the 1930s, the Gerber House was used as the school's infirmary. The basement was also used to store coffins and bodies during the wintertime for the Catholic church. Since the ground was usually frozen solid, the dead were kept in the cold basement until springtime. This could explain why there are so many shadow figures hanging around this area. They could be parasite spirits that were brought in long ago when the bodies were there.

On a lighter note, I have encountered a couple different ghosts in this area, including those of former students and Christian Gerber himself (although that encounter was very brief). One of the more interesting things I witnessed in the basement occurred when the local TOGHS ghost hunting team placed a bunch of REM pods around the room. After calling on the spirits to do something, the REM pods began going off one by one, as if the ghost was running around the room setting them off.

Third Wing Basement

If you want to truly experience the paranormal, you need to visit the third wing basement, which is located off the main entrance, and just sit there for an hour. This room was used by St. Vincent's Hospital as a drug rehab center before it was turned into a black box theater in 2017. This basement

Chris Bores sitting on the Gerber House steps, waiting for his tour group to arrive. *Chris Bores*.

In the back-righthand corner of the Gerber House basement, one resident saw a shadow person disappear into the wall. *Chris Bores*.

is hands down the most haunted area in the building. It was also the one area where I could always get the spirits to interact with me on command. This was so amazing, because whenever we had big financial donors come in to experience the paranormal, I could always count on the spirits to put on a good show if I took the donors down there.

The first time I went into the basement on May 10, 2014, I had a tour group with me. I pulled out my K2 meter and called out to the empty room, "If there is anyone down here, can you touch that meter, please?"

The meter spiked.

"Can you do that again? I just want to make sure someone is actually doing that."

Another spike occurred.

"Can you bring that up to the third light there?"

The spirit complied. My tour group all stood in shock. "Can you touch this meter if we can have a yes no session with you?"

The meter stopped reacting. No.

Would you like us to leave?"

Yes.

"You don't want us in this room right now?"

Yes.

"Are we upsetting you?"

The meter spiked hard for several seconds. I instantly felt an odd electrical sensation surround me. "Man, that is solid red!" I told the crowd. "All right, tell you what. We'll leave if you make a noise for us."

We waited for a few seconds, and nothing happened. Sticking around at this point was probably a jerk move, but I was just starting out as a tour guide and was hungry for more interaction.

"Can you knock on that table?"

No response.

"Do you not want us to leave?"

No response.

"If you want, I can help you. Do you want me to help you move on?"

No response.

"You do not want me to help you move on?"

At last, we got a spike.

"What era did you live in? The '60s?"

No reply.

"The '70s?"

No reply.

The Evil Presence

Even though I loved talking to all the ghosts at Collingwood, there was one I always hated encountering. Every time this nasty thing came into the room, it would scare off all the other spirits. You could feel its dark energy roll into the area. The first time I encountered this force, I was in the Burn Room. The room at one point felt like it was getting darker as the spirit moved in. This was a small taste of what this entity could really do when given the chance.

About one year later, on October 26, 2014, I had a huge group in the basement. We were having a very pleasant conversation with a ghost until two ladies came down and started getting quite belligerent with their questions, causing a shift in the conversation. After a brief silence, the meters lit up in a way I'd never seen before. They were spiking in ten-second intervals and then stopped after a minute or two. A few moments later, the cycle restarted over again. This went on for quite some time. Was the spirit annoyed? Upset? I had no idea. I tried asking, but it was no use. The weird spiking pattern continued. I then asked, "Are there certain spirits here we should be afraid of?" That's when things took a dark turn.

Instantly, the meters fell silent to my question.

This was the first time in over five minutes they had stopped spiking. About a minute later, one by one, the people in my tour group began mentioning how cold it was getting. I reached out my hand and walked around the room. I could definitely feel cold spots forming around us. Without warning, one of the K2 meters on the chair went off. It was a steady spike that started with one light appearing, then two and then three. The spikes were visually building in intensity. Shortly after that, the second K2 meter also spiked the exact same way. One light, two lights and then three. I had never encountered this spiking pattern ever before. It came with an overwhelming feeling that something dark and sinister was slowly rolling into the area.

I began looking around the room. It was getting darker by the second. The faint red exit light illuminating the doorway on the far side of the room slowly faded into the darkness surrounding it. This dark energy was sucking all the light away as it rolled in. I looked back at the K2 meters. Both of them held steady at three lights, which never wavered. Was this to signify the number three that demons are known to mock God with?

Suddenly, my tour group began exclaiming that they were seeing shadows dart past them and around the room. More people began seeing the same thing. I then saw a brief flash of light flicker behind a pillar that I couldn't explain. We also heard the faint sound of a woman screaming in the distance. Activity exploded all around us.

Then as quickly as it started, it came to a screeching halt. The K2 meters slowly decreased in intensity, and the dark feeling in the room dissipated along with it. Whatever rolled in had rolled right back out.

A month later, I encountered the dark presence again when I was in the basement trying an experiment called "Charlie, Charlie." This is a game in which you set up two pencils in a yes/no formation on a piece of paper. The experiment failed miserably, but the K2 meters I placed around the board acted strangely.

"Do you want violence?" I asked.

The meters spiked hard for the first time that evening. Yes.

"Do you want us to kill someone?"

Yes.

That reply spooked me a bit. I'm not sure where that darn entity came from, but I hope I never have to find out.

There have been times when some of these nasty entities have actually followed people home. One of the ghost hunters I usually worked with, Scott Mahoney, ended up having a creepy encounter at his house after we had an amazing interaction with the evil presence the previous night. Scott and his wife were at home that evening and suddenly heard a hissing sound coming from a dark room behind them. The hissing occurred three or four times in succession.

I also had something follow me home after I made a visit to the Collingwood building in 2022 to meet up with our photographer friend. After leaving, I forgot to cleanse myself from the energy of the place. A few days later, I was jolted awake in the early morning to see a dark, tall, lanky gremlin-looking thing running back and forth in our bedroom while grunting. I quickly called upon Archangel Michael to help remove that thing from our house, and I had to purify our living space afterward.

Caroline

The teenage girl named Caroline is said to hang out around the first-floor bathroom next to the classrooms. She was the first spirit I really got to interact with at Collingwood on May 10, 2014. I had my first tour group in tow, and I placed my K2 meter down on the sink basin.

"Caroline, if you're in here, can you spike this meter for me?"

The meter began spiking.

"Are you a little girl? Touch that meter if you are."

Yes.

"Caroline, can you make a noise for us, please?"

Everyone stood silently. Suddenly, a loud noise from the hallway broke the silence. It sounded like someone had slammed their fist down on a bench as hard as they could.

"That sounded like the side of the bench!" Elaine in my tour group exclaimed.

"Caroline—" I said with astonishment. I walked out into the hallway and examined the bench. There was nothing on it, near it or even around it that would have made a sound like that. "Caroline, is that you?"

The meter went nuts. Yes.

"Can you back away from the meter, please?"

She complied.

"Was that you that made a knock on this bench earlier?"

Yes.

I walked into the bathroom to grab my meters out of there and instantly felt cold spots forming all around me. "Oh man, I'm getting chills again. You're right here, aren't you?" I extended my hand outward and felt a sudden drop in temperature. It was isolated within small pockets. "Do you want us to pray for you?"

Yes.

"Do you need help moving on?"

No.

"Are you stuck where you are?"

Yes.

"Was it because of something you did while you were alive?"

No.

I find it truly amazing that spirits want prayers. Many times, when I ask a spirit if they want us to pray for them, they say yes. This response shows that prayers have an effect on ghosts that we do not fully comprehend.

"Is it hard for you to give me your name?"

Yes.

"Do you want us to leave?"

No.

"Are you having fun with us?"

Yes.

The response elicited laughter from everyone in the room. "Do you miss the residents at the facility here?" I asked because the administrators of the building had just kicked them all out.

No.

"Do you like having the place to yourself?"

Yes.

"Do you get frustrated that sometimes people can't hear you talk?"

Yes.

This conversation continued for at least sixty minutes, which is unheard of in this field. You can view the entire video on my *Ghost Doctor* YouTube channel, because I got into more heady topics that are too expansive to address here. Caroline was fun to talk to, but unfortunately, I was never able to find her again. As I continued to work at Collingwood, I always wondered what happened to her. I only hope that my prayers helped her move on to a better place.

The Students

Many times, I was able to interact with a few students from when the building was used as a school. The one student who loved interacting with me hung out in the Gerber House basement. The following is a string of conversations that started on August 22, 2014.

"Do you want me to bring a food offering down here for you?"

No.

"Do you want us to bring you anything?"

Yes.

"Do you need prayers?"

No.

"Do you need help moving on?

No.

"Were you a nun here?"

No.

"Were you a student?"

Yes.

"Were you a student of the St. Ursula Academy?"

Yes.

"Or were you a student of Mary Manse College?"

No.

"So, you were a student of St. Ursula?

Yes.

"Were you female?"

Yes.

"Were you male?"

No.

"So, you were female?"

Yes.

"Sorry for the redundant questions. I just want to make sure. Did you live during the 1920s?"

No.

I ran through all the decades. The meter spiked when I got to the '70s.

"OK, neat! So, the 1970s, with the peace and love and the Beatles and all that?"

Yes.

"And you died near here?"

Yes.

"I'm kind of curious why you still hang around this building. Did you really like it here?"

Yes.

"So, if you lived in the '70s, did you also die in the '70s?"

The meter spiked for a long time. It was a huge yes.

"Were you a teenager when you passed away?"

No.

"Were you over the age of eighteen?"

Yes.

"Were you in your twenties?"

Yes.

"Did it take you a longtime to figure out you had passed away?"

Yes.

"Were you confused for a while?"

No.

"Did you die in the wintertime?"

Yes.

"I'm trying to figure out who you are. Do you know if it was in January?"

No response.

"February?"

No response.

"Are you still here with us?

No response.

I hate it when they do that. I got into the same line of questioning with this student a few times afterward, and whenever I tried pinpointing when she died, she wouldn't give me an answer. So, either she doesn't know, or the answer causes her too much pain to recall.

During my five years working at the Collingwood Arts Center, I learned and experienced a lot, and it helped further my success in the paranormal field. Unfortunately, toward the end of my tenure, another local ghost hunter deviously pushed me out of Collingwood, as he weaseled his way in. It's sad to see ego win the day, especially at the expense of the spirits. After I was pushed out, the ghosts grew very abrasive, and the tours became very negative. This occurred for a while until things tapered off greatly. It's a shame to see the activity level drop off so much, especially since they seemed so delighted to interact with me over the years. Being able to pull the spirits out for my tour groups was a joy for both guests and spirits alike. It is a time I will never forget.

3

TOLEDO EXPRESS AIRPORT

O ne might not think that a place like the Toledo Express Airport is haunted without witnessing the activity firsthand. I even had my doubts when I was first called in to help the staff. It wasn't until after I conducted my investigation that the activity itself made me a believer. Once I dug into the airport's history, I understood why the site was so haunted.

The Toledo Airport opened in 1954 to replace the previous smaller Toledo Executive Airport in southern Toledo. Throughout the 1980s and '90s, the airport went through quite a boom period, as it picked up major airlines to accommodate commercial planes, private corporate planes and military planes. When it came time to dig into the airport's tragic past, I found that it's had quite the history.

The first and most famous of the airport's plane crashes occurred on October 29, 1960. An airplane carrying the entire California State Polytechnic University football team took off during a dense fog in which the visibility was zero. The plane lifted up, failed to gain altitude and nosedived back into the ground, killing sixteen players and eight other passengers.

On July 7, 1971, a second crash occurred when a twin-engine plane carrying a huge cargo of mail lifted up and also failed to gain altitude. After slamming back onto the ground, it blew up in a fiery explosion, killing both pilots, James Fugate and John Pierce, and destroying 1,900 pounds of mail.

On February 15, 1992, a Douglas DC-8 military cargo plane landed in a nearby wheat field three miles away from the runway when the captain became "spatially disorientated." All four crew members aboard were killed.

The Toledo Express Airport in 1964. *Toledo Public Library*.

The aftermath of the mail-carrying airplane that crashed in 1971. The burned wreckage sits in a pool of foam in the middle of the east-west runway. *From the* Toledo Blade.

On April 8, 2003, a military Dassault Falcon 20 descended during icy conditions, causing the landing configuration to malfunction. The plane crash landed, killing two pilots and a passenger.

When it comes to haunted activity at this location, the night crew seems to experience most of it. Back in the control room, they often feel like they are being watched and hear odd noises throughout the night. In the air traffic control tower, workers sometimes hear footsteps coming up the stairs. When they turn around to look, the hallway is empty. The staff's break room is also where crew members have heard unexplained voices and seen shadowy figures. In the lounge room, the staff has seen an apparition of a woman late at night. Other times, lights turn on and off by themselves. The woman has also been seen in the surrounding hallways. Crew members have also heard her voice and smelled her perfume. They have also seen shadows figures darting around.

My Investigation

For any ghost hunter, being granted access to such a sensitive area like a working airport is a once-in-a-lifetime event. A quick internet search reveals that no one has ever pulled it off aside from me. I got a call from the Toledo Airport's night crew in 2017, asking me for help since they heard of my work as a ghost behaviorist. They had been experiencing paranormal disturbances for a while, but things had escalated and were happening on a nightly basis. They were looking for someone to come in and help clear the air.

When I arrived, I met with Dan. He walked me through the airport terminal and took me behind the sacred door labeled "No Entry." I was awestruck by all the instruments in the various rooms, hidden away from public eyes. I was like a little kid, eyes wide and asking many questions. Dan explained to me that their haunting was pretty routine over the years, but for some reason, things were beginning to happen almost nightly.

As he showed me around, we heard a pair of headphones fall off the wall from the hook they were hanging from. We looked at each other, saying, "Did that really just fall off that by itself?" Sadly, my camera wasn't even turned on yet to document it.

I quickly set up shop in the lower airport control room. I placed a wide variety of tools across the desk. I even brought one of my colleagues, Scott Mahoney, who assisted me at the Collingwood Arts Center many times. I was determined to get answers for Dan, so I spent the first few minutes trying to get the spirits acclimated with my presence. I soon began getting spikes on my K2 meter.

"Can you do that again?" I asked.

The spirit complied.

"There you go!" Before I could ask another question, my Ovilus ghost device (otherwise known as a voice box for the dead) went off and spit out a word: *eat*.

I wondered if this spirit was hungry. "Are you hungry? Do you want some peanut butter? Spike that meter if you do."

The meter spiked instantly. Yes.

"OK!" I enthusiastically exclaimed. One of the things I like to do is perform what I call a food offering. Food offerings have been performed for centuries in various religions, especially during the celebration of the Mexican Day of the Dead celebration. I often bring a jar of peanut butter with me because the scent is very strong, and I find ghosts can feed off it to acquire a sort of spiritual currency that helps in some way.

"All right, let me ask you a question. Did you use to work here?"

No.

"Were you a passenger of a plane?"

Yes.

"Did you die around here?"

Yes.

Prior to arriving, I had found a list of names of all the people who died in the 1960s airplane crash. While reading them off, none of them had elicited any type of a response. So, that ruled out that this ghost originated from that crash.

"Are you male?" I asked.

No response.

"Are you female?"

No response.

"Do you not know what you are?"

No response.

"Are you confused?"

At last, the meter spiked. Yes.

This was interesting. I find that spirits can become foggy with the details of their death and even who they are if they died so suddenly. Working through the pain of those tragic events can cause many types of coping disorders to manifest, which takes years to sort out in the afterlife.

"Were you a passenger on an airplane?"

Yes.

"Was it a jet airliner?"

Yes.

"Did you work for the military?"

Yes.

"Do you have any affiliation with this place?"

Yes.

Suddenly, Dan chimed in with some important information that was unknown to us. "One plane crash that happened up here was a heavy DC-8 military aircraft. There was one passenger. I don't know what the guy's name was."

Upon hearing this, I turned to address the spirit. "Are you him?"

Yes.

The answer not only exploded onto the K2 meter, but everyone in the room felt a surge of electrical energy slice through the air like a lightning bolt.

"Whoa!" I shouted as I felt this odd electric rush jolt up my body. It was so intense.

Even Scott, who was sitting across the room, was overcome with the odd sensation. "I've got goose bumps! What was that?"

I knew the spirit was very happy that we had connected the dots correctly to figure out his backstory. "Well, it's been what—twenty-one years?" I said

Chris makes contact with the 1992 airplane crash victim during an investigation. *Chris Bores*.

to bring the spirit up to speed. "So, you've been hanging around here for twenty-one years."

The meter spiked very intensely.

"Yeah, it's been twenty-one years there. So, you were involved in that crash, correct?"

No response.

"Correct?" I asked again.

Nothing.

Scott jumped in. "Is that a touchy subject? Was it sad?"

Yes.

"Oh, you're sad." I stated. Well, that made perfect sense. "Are you still working through that? The tragedy of that?"

Yes.

"Do you want me to pray for you? Do you need prayers?"

Yes.

"OK, I will pray for you. I know sometimes it takes a while to work through this stuff, especially where you're at. Where you're able to manipulate all kinds of energies and get caught up in your own mind and manifestations. Am I correct?

The meter spiked wildly. Yes.

"So, are you male?"

No.

"Were you female?"

Yes.

"So, you were female? Just so I know."

Yes.

The session pretty much ran its course and tapered off shortly thereafter. I hadn't considered bringing any prayer tools, so I needed to come back for a second visit. Once I got home, I found the details of this 1992 DC-8 airplane crash online. The odd thing I noticed was that a woman wasn't listed as a passenger on the plane. So, where did the female spirit fit into all this?

A month later, I returned to the airport, armed with the printout of the DC-8 crash information. I hoped that by reading it out loud, it would bring the woman back so I could continue our discussion. I started by reading from the crash log. As I read, the meter began subtly spiking.

"Hey there! Are you the captain? Can you spike the meter?"

The meter spiked. Yes.

"Can you do that again for me, please? Are you the captain?"

Yes.

Not only did the meter spike, but the Ovilus went off, too: *story*.

"Whoa, check that out! Yeah, I was just telling your story!" I exclaimed. So, you were the captain?"

Yes.

"Was there a woman on your flight?"

No.

"Were you the woman we talked to last time?"

No.

This was very confusing. Was there another crash I didn't know about? Thankfully, Dan jumped in and told us about another crash he had forgotten about that occurred in 2003.

My mouth hung open. "Wow, so that's who we were probably talking to last time then. And the only reason this captain spirit [from the 1992 crash] probably started conversing with us is because we started talking about his crash on this printout. Correct?"

Yes.

"Are you currently working through your situation?"

No.

"Are you happy where you are?"

Yes.

"So, your happy here?"

Yes.

This was incredible. The woman spirit we talked to the last time told us she was sad. This new spirit, on the other hand, was happy. "Does it frustrate you sometimes that people can't hear you talk?"

Yes.

"Do you want us to say a little prayer for you before we leave?"

Yes.

I soon began going through my ritual of chanting mantras and ringing bells for the spirit. Both meters exploded to life throughout the process. Whatever I had done seemed to work. I tried to get more interactions afterward, but my meters remained silent.

My time at the Toledo Airport was amazing. Hopefully, the activity quieted down after that. The crew never called me back, so I can only assume they finally got a bit of relief from the spirits haunting them.

4

TOLEDO ZOO

Have you ever traveled to the Toledo Zoo and felt like it was haunted? I know I didn't, but if you talk to their employees, they'll tell you they've had many unusual experiences late at night. Digging into the history of the zoo revealed not only why the place is haunted, but also a hidden piece of history about a particular Walbridge Park area that used to be part of the zoo.

In 1895, Walbridge Park opened along the shoreline just east of where the Toledo Zoo now sits. The park contained a pavilion, greenhouses, bathhouses and a beach on the shore. In 1899, the park was expanding, and decided to build a zoo. The first animal donated to the cause was a woodchuck, which the zoo promptly put on display. More donations slowly arrived, and by the end of the year, the zoo had amassed thirty-nine animals, including black bears, alligators and an owl. The year 1904 saw the addition of a sea lion pool, while in 1911, the circus graciously donated lions, elephants and zebras. By the 1920s, Walbridge Park had grown to comprise thirty acres in size with a full-fledged Amusement Park Midway right off the beach. There was a dance hall, a figure-eight roller coaster, bumper cars, a shooting gallery, a fun house, a merry-go-round, restaurants, concession stands and more. In 1927, the park purchased thirty-six acres of land for the zoo to expand into. It constructed six animal buildings and an amphitheater to become the second-largest zoo in animal displays in the country behind the Bronx Zoo by 1939.

Walbridge Park attracted tourists from all over the state. It was very popular. Unfortunately, it met its untimely demise on October 26, 1938,

The Toledo Zoo entrance sign. *Chris Bores.*

when a huge fire broke out and spread quickly, burning down most of the Midway. The park sadly went up in flames, and after that night, all attention shifted to the zoo as it rebranded itself as the Toledo Zoo.

When it comes to the haunted side of things, activity seems to happen in the animal buildings. According to security guard Brock Manyon, "I worked there for ten years alone overnight. It's definitely haunted." He explained that he spent long hours in the amphitheater, aquarium and birdhouse and has had many experiences ranging from hearing unexplained noises, feeling that he was being watched and seeing shadow figures.

The most haunted building at the zoo, according to employees, is the Museum of Science (now called the Museum of Natural History). According to Wanda Davis, "Before they renovated the museum, I was working in there, cleaning. Several different times, I would hear people talking late at night, but I knew I was the only one in the building cleaning it. Many times, I heard music and a man and a woman upstairs laughing and talking. One time, I seen a black figure of a man just floating in the hall where the Great Hall used to be. At first, I wasn't sure what I saw, but it happened two other times!"

I myself recall feeling a strange heaviness in the museum when I visited in the past. I could never put my finger on what it was, but after hearing the place is haunted, it made perfect sense.

Larry Devaughn was a custodian who worked there from 2007 to 2012. He added, "I heard doors slam and lights go out as I walked by when no one

Walbridge Park Pavilion, 1900. *Toledo Public Library*.

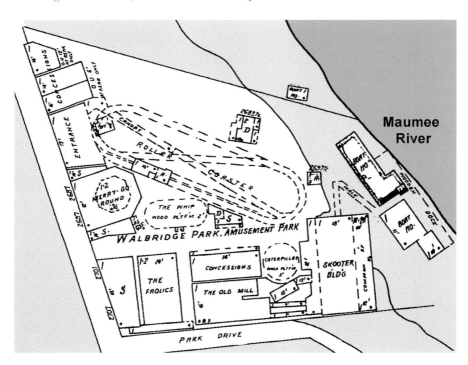

Zoo Walbridge Park, park map, 1932. *Toledo Public Library*.

Walbridge Park Midway, 1910s. *Toledo Public Library*.

else was there." One morning, he ended up having an encounter that really unnerved him. "I arrived at the zoo at 5:30 a.m. and went upstairs to the balcony. A ceiling light flashed on and off; then the door below the light just slammed shut. I checked the offices, and there was no one inside!"

Even a friend of mine who currently works at the zoo has also said that she's heard many other firsthand accounts of ghostly experiences from her coworkers. So, something is definitely going on there.

While researching to see if anyone died at either the Toledo Zoo or Walbridge Park, I came up with a huge list of names. First, I found several people who drowned along the coastline of Walbridge Park's beaches. This included George Hirth in 1901 and Bessie Royce in 1911. Then there is a wild case from 1905 in which the body of Jessica Coy washed up on shore a week after Abby Willing's body had washed up. Both were deemed drownings by police until a third body, that of Ella Graybill, washed up a week later. Police thought they had a serial killer on their hands until they found out Ella had died by suicide after her boyfriend, George Benninger, beat her regularly.

At the Toledo Zoo, zookeeper Michael Raditz was killed in 1914, when he was working at an elephant riding station. He put a saddle on an elephant, causing it to freak out and impale him with its giant elephant tusks. Over seven hundred people saw the tragedy unfold. In 1929, zookeeper C. Connor was mauled to death by two zebras while working in their cage. Then on January 19, 1972, nineteen-year-old Richard Hale visited the zoo while

Top: The aftermath of the Walbridge Park fire in 1938. *Toledo Public Library*.

Bottom: The elephant attraction where a zookeeper was impaled by an elephant's tusk. *Toledo Public Library*.

Opposite: The Polar Bear Grotto, where Richard Hale died, in 1972. The arrow points to where the zookeepers later found his body. It was previously located where the Tiger Terrace now sits, on the corner of the first left path from the bridge. *From the* Toledo Blade.

high on the drug methadone and wandered over to the polar bears' grotto exhibit. He climbed over the guardrail, crossed six feet of lawn and dropped fourteen feet into the moat below. The polar bears attacked and mauled him to death. His body was found later that day, floating in the moat. According to previous zoo director Philip Skeldon, the body was "pretty eaten up. The legs and everything was just bone. It was a gruesome sight."

The last documented death, that of a five-year-old boy visiting from Smith Road Elementary, occurred in 2011. His kindergarten class took a field trip, and the young boy complained of a belly ache before collapsing onto the ground in the tunnel. A nearby doctor administered CPR, but it was of no use. He died, and the cause of death was never publicly released.

When it comes to zoo hauntings, it seems that the ghosts also like to haunt the surrounding houses close by. According to Holly Clark Burgete, "We lived right by the zoo when I was four years old. We had to move because my mom saw me talking to someone. She was a little girl that wore a blue dress and had blond hair with ribbons in it."

Rita Cope also added, "I know someone who lived close to the zoo, and their kitchen cabinet doors used to fly open all the time. One time, a rocking chair in a bedroom was rocking all by itself."

The Carnivora House is one of the six animal buildings the Toledo Zoo built throughout the 1930s. *Toledo Public Library.*

Shavaun Andrews also remembered, "I lived on Dartmouth right by the Toledo Zoo. Many nights, I could hear footsteps in our attic. One night, the footsteps came down the steps, and my bedroom door flung open."

It's amazing to know that a place I visited hundreds of times has its own ghosts haunting and I didn't even know about it. Hopefully, the restless spirits can find peace one day and move on to where they need to go.

5

SPAGHETTI WAREHOUSE

The land at 42 South Superior Street may be home to the Spaghetti Warehouse now, but it has a long past that seems to attract the paranormal. The location was first used as the Eddy, Avery, and Eddy's Lumber Yard in the mid-1880s. That company sold the land to Hoppe and Strub, which built a Pabst Blue Ribbon bottling factory there in 1897. The building became Lee Chas Industry in the 1930s, then City Produce and Poultry in the 1940s, Lee's Storage Co. in 1952 and finally the Spaghetti Warehouse Italian restaurant in 1976. Once the restaurant opened for business, both costumers and workers alike began feeling the presence of ghosts.

The hauntings seem to occur all throughout the three-story building. According to B. Bailey, "My wife is a psychic. There are two hauntings with a man and woman from different time periods there. The guy was killed in a freak accident many, many years ago. The woman, she wasn't sure about."

My own research into the Spaghetti Warehouse hauntings support Bailey's claims, since all the stories either center around a male and female spirit. After interviewing many employees of the Spaghetti Warehouse, it seems the female spirit likes to haunt the main restaurant. She likes pulling pranks, like moving objects around the room, including dishes, silverware, glasses, chairs and place settings. Sometimes, when the staff arrives to work in the morning, they are greeted with a mess. According to Tara, "I closed the restaurant one Sunday. We cleaned everything before leaving. When I arrived on Monday, my manager was upset because chairs were everywhere, and sugar packets covered the floor."

The Spaghetti Warehouse as it stands today. *Chris Bores*.

The Hoppe and Strub Bottling Company, where they made Pabst beer, in 1900. *Toledo Public Library*.

An old trolley from the early 1900s is worked into the restaurant's floor plan and sits in the center of the room. Some feel that this old relic has a spirit attached to it. According to previous hostess Cathy Silvis, "Every time I walked around the other side of the trolley, I heard a woman's voice, and she was whispering. I opened every Sunday, so it was usually quiet."

As for customers who dine in, they sometimes feel unexplained taps on their shoulders or tugging on their hair. Some even feel like they are being watched by an unseen presence.

When it comes to the male spirit, he haunts the entire building, but his presence is mostly felt in the basement. People have felt cold spots, like they are being watched and a heaviness to the air. I visited in 2013 and went downstairs to use the bathroom. At the time, I had no idea the building was haunted, but I could feel something was in the room, watching me.

Kitchen worker Roger Green shared, "There was a lady going to the bathroom, and she came upstairs saying she seen a guy with a mustache." I even found a story from 2002 about two other women who also saw a man appear in front of them, walk into the far wall and disappear.

The current bartender told me she hates going down into the basement storage room alone, because many times, she'll start feeling someone breathing on the back of her neck.

Customer Peggy Curran shared, "After dinner, my daughter and I took the grandchildren to the gaming area downstairs. My grandson, who was two years old, kept staring toward the back of the room in the bar area. He would run toward the dark part of the room and then run back to his mom, smiling. When we were leaving, he looked back in the dark room and said, 'Bye Tony.' I swear this is a true story."

Employee Jodi Cole also feels the haunted activity almost daily. "Some days, I get a feeling something is watching me. When I go into the basement, I get this uneasy feeling. One day, the storeroom light came on by itself. Yesterday, in the freezer, the bread just came crashing down." She also told me that a fellow coworker had quit her job recently because she had used the basement restroom and heard the stall door open by itself and a ghostly voice call out her name.

General manager Dean Pickett is no stranger to his employee's telling him about the ghostly things that happen to them. "People often report seeing shadows and people that shouldn't be there."

Even the levels above the restaurant, which are used for storage, are said to be haunted. Worker Kelly Kromenacker said, "After closing, we would hear chairs moving up on the second floor. None of us would dare go up

A trolley sits in the center of the restaurant. A few waitresses have heard ghostly female voices around this area. *Chris Bores*.

there!" The staff also hears footsteps when no one is up there. Another waitress went up to the second floor one evening to grab something out of storage. She witnessed a wicker basket levitate and hover a bit before slowly lowering back down again. On another occasion, another waitress heard her name being called out from the darkness on the other side of the room.

Su Lasko Massey also recalled, "When it's quiet, you can hear stuff throughout the rooms moving that shouldn't be. I used to go sit and wait [to pick up my friend] at closing time because she'd get so freaked out."

The Spaghetti Warehouse's security guards also get no relief from the activity. Shayaun Andrews explained, "A security officer was working late, and the manager was in the basement counting money. The security officer came out of the kitchen and saw a woman sitting up front by the window. He couldn't see her well because the trolley was in the way. He moved to get a better look and said she was wearing period clothes. She turned her head to look at him and vanished."

In 2021, local ghost hunter Al Luna began conducting public ghost tours at the Spaghetti Warehouse. He brought in his team psychic, who was able to get a few names from the spirits. The psychic claimed the woman is named Sally, while the man is named Christopher. As for pulling out other details for their lives, Luna explained, "They are not real good about divulging much about their lives. What I've got from them is they were born in the

In the Spaghetti Warehouse basement, people have felt like they were being watched, and a few have even seen an apparition of the man haunting this building. *Chris Bores*.

mid- to late 1800s. Sally had an association with the Pabst bottling company in the building. Christopher is not giving up any secrets."

While doing some deep digging, I was able to find that a man named Charles Leak had died at the location on December 24, 1905. Since the name Charles is very close to Christopher, I can't help but wonder if that could be the real name of the mystery man who is haunting the restaurant.

My Investigation

During the Halloween season of 2017, I was asked by WTOL's news channel 11 to do a ghost hunting segment with them at the Spaghetti Warehouse. I showed up with all my ghost gadgets and started walking around the restaurant. I came up empty-handed. I then descended into the basement and pulled out my Ovilus device. This item takes the energy in an area and converts it into words. I called out to the empty room, "What is this room used for?" I waited a few seconds and surprisingly received a word: *eat*.

This was pretty much dead on. That is exactly what the room was used for. I headed into the basement storage room next. I instantly saw why everyone hated going into this area alone to retrieve items. The brick-walled room gave me a creepy vibe, since it had that unfinished basement look harkening

Chris gets a slight interaction with the man in the second-story storage area with his K2 meter. *Chris Bores.*

back to the 1800s. I used a variety of tools for spirit detection, but nothing happened. All I felt was an odd sensation hanging in the air.

We then headed to the second-floor storage room. "Can you spike my meter, please? I really want to communicate with you."

Nothing happened.

I then decided to use a psychological ploy, using the woman news reporter as leverage. I often find that male ghosts respond better when enticing them with a pretty lady. "Do you want to talk to Ida? She's the news reporter."

Finally, the meter spiked.

"Oh, yeah? Do you like having Ida here?"

The K2 meter lit up again. Yes.

Ida laughed at the immediate response. She couldn't believe it.

I asked a few more questions, but the conversation ended pretty quickly. He was indeed tight-lipped. I'm still not sure who exactly haunts this building, but there is definitely a male presence lurking about.

6

Repertoire Theater

The Repertoire Theatre at 16 Tenth Street has seen its fair share of haunted activity over the years. And the history of this location begins in the late 1800s, when it was a row of residential houses facing Washington Street. One of those homes belonged to the Sullivans. On May 25, 1906, their seven-year-old daughter, Mary Ann Sullivan, ran out into the street at the Washington Street crosswalk. A streetcar then slammed into her and dragged her body one hundred feet down the street, as it was pinned underneath the front tire. Everyone aboard cried at the sight before them. After the accident, the Sullivans were so distraught, they sold their home in 1907 to the First Friendship Baptist Church. The church built a chapel on the land. In 1946, the building was sold off and converted into the current Repertoire Theater. Since then, the building has become home to a few spirits that are attached to the land, including Mary.

The Basement

The basement is reported to be the most haunted location, where things either turn up missing or are moved around the room. It is believed that Mary is behind these playful acts, since a few people have seen the apparition of a little blond-haired girl in this area. Everything that turns up missing is instantly associated with this spirit. She is very playful, and on very rare occasions, someone hears her giggling.

Toledo Public Library.

One incident happened with the theater's maintenance man when he couldn't find his keys. They were lost for a few days until they reappeared in the locked light control room, which he never had access to. Theater manager Bonnie Herrmann also lost a box of Girl Scout cookies when she brought them in for a fellow coworker. She left them on the table before leaving one night, and by the next morning, the box had disappeared. They've never turned up since. So, it seems like Mary loves cookies.

Local ghost hunter Chris Tillman came in to investigate the haunting one evening and caught the EVP of Mary saying the word *Mommy*.

Theater manager Bonnie Herrmann said whenever she works downstairs, she'll often hear ghostly footsteps of someone walking around in the theater above. "I hear footsteps all the time, especially when we have the more elaborate production sets. One time, all I could hear was running back and forth across the stage. It was so loud, I had to yell upstairs for them to stop." Thankfully, whenever she tells the ghosts to do something, they comply.

Even though most of the hauntings are playful and pleasant, there was one that was quite the opposite. "I was here by myself in my office past 11:00 p.m. I had this really scary feeling come over me, to the point where I had to call my husband. I felt like I was being watched. I was just working, and it felt like someone was standing over me and judging me." When her husband arrived, the odd feeling dissipated.

Above: The Repertoire Theater, 1965. *Toledo Public Library*.

Right: Anna Sullivan would have lived in a house very similar to this one. This house stood down the street at 120 Tenth Street. *Toledo Public Library*.

The Theater

The main theater is where a mysterious well-dressed man appears. Many times, stage builders working on the set design late at night have looked out into the empty rows of seats and seen this ghostly apparition sitting there, just watching the stage. People often see him in the very back on the left-hand side of the theater. Other times, he is sitting in the center of the middle aisle. This ghostly gentleman has also been spotted in the lobby. He's appeared so many times, the staff has named him George.

The stage area is home to other hauntings as well. A theater director who was doing rehearsals one evening heard power tools coming from behind the stage. Since she was the only person there, it freaked her out, and she left for the night. Other reports include people feeling weird tugs on their clothing or smelling incense. This is interesting, since the stage was the exact location of the altar when the building was a Baptist church.

Upstairs Office

The upstairs office area is said to be haunted by a lady in white. Whenever people see her apparition, she is wearing a white dress and is around twenty years of age. She mostly interacts with people late at night when they are about to head out of the office. That's when they'll hear a female voice call out, "Turn off the lights, please." This happens very frequently.

A few others have also reported being in the parking lot and seeing her apparition when they look up at the window of the upstairs office.

While digging into the theater's past, I found that a woman named Mary Steward died at this very location in 1889. Could she be the source of this haunting?

The Brown Building

The last area reported to be haunted is in a building located on the other side of the parking lot, which is also owned by the Repertoire Theater. Nicknamed the Brown Building, the theater uses the downstairs area as a workshop, while the upstairs area is used as a costume shop. Thousands of outfits are housed in this location for the actors. It seems that a few uninvited spirits are also hanging out here. Manager Bonnie Herrmann explained,

Top: A figure of a man is usually seen sitting in the back-left corner of the theater seating area. The figure has also appeared in the middle seating section as well. *Chris Bores*.

Bottom: The Brown House was supposedly haunted until a side wall of the building caved in. Once it was replaced, the dark energy moved on. *Chris Bores*.

"We had something nasty in our Brown Building. I would not go up into the costume shop by myself. It was too scary." She then told me about an incident that occurred a few years ago, when a ghost hunting group came in and a member was scratched on the arm. Negative things kept happening to visitors until one day in 2019, a side wall collapsed in on itself. After being repaired, the energy of the building shifted. "I don't feel it there anymore," said Herrmann. "I'll go up there by myself now."

MY INVESTIGATION

I arrived at the Repertoire Theater with my spiritual medium friend Marie, who I hoped could sense more than I could just by walking through. As we made our way to the main theater, Marie instantly felt a male presence. She felt his name wasn't George, like they had nicknamed him. Unfortunately, she wasn't able to sense his real name or backstory.

As we ascended the stairs to the third-floor office and prop room area, things became more interesting. Theater manager Bonnie was standing there, telling me about how the lady in white often is heard telling people to "turn off the lights" upon leaving. During this conversation, I had my tape recorder running. As soon as she finished telling me her story, I caught an EVP of a teenage girl snidely remarking, "So what!" After hearing this voice and sharing it with the manager, we both believe that the lady in white probably isn't a lady at all, but a feisty teenager in white.

Marie arrived moments later. She instantly remarked, "It's definitely heavy up here! I can definitely feel her in here." With that confirmation, I'm confident in saying that EVP came from our lady in white.

Later on, I was able to bring in more ghost hunting equipment and conduct a proper investigation. I decided to perform an SB7 session. While trying to ask for a name, I caught a female saying the name Teresa. I cannot 100 percent confirm that Teresa is the lady in white's actual name, but I definitely feel like her past is tied to the period when the building was a chapel.

Marie also sensed another presence in that area of a male that was strong and very overpowering. A rush of unwelcome energy washed over her, revealing that he did not like us poking around there. Many other medium type-sensitives have also felt the same in the prop room.

Finally, it was time to tackle the basement. Marie quickly made contact with the young girl. She turned out to be a bit very apprehensive.

"She's really shy. I think she's embarrassed. She feels silly about what happened with the streetcar accident. I think she was chasing after a ball and ran out into the street after it. She feels stupid." After hearing that, I told

Mary that she didn't have to feel embarrassed. It was a mistake, and people make them all the time. Marie felt like Mary came from a period from when the building was used as her home.

Later, I returned to that area with more ghost hunting gear in tow in the hopes of breaking the ice with her a bit. After spending about fifteen minutes building a suitable level of comfort with Mary, I pulled out a modified music box that had been recalibrated to start playing music whenever a spirit walks in front of it. I placed it on a nearby table and showed her how to use it. To my amazement, it only took about a minute for her to start setting the toy off in two or three split-second intervals.

"Is that you?" I asked.

The music box went off again.

"Do you like that? Walk in front of it again."

She compiled, but the spikes were very brief.

I asked a few more questions, but there were no further responses from Mary. "Can you walk in front of it again?"

Almost instantly, the device chimed to life.

"So, do you like being here?"

"Yes," she implied by spiking the meter.

"Do you like cookies? Do you want me to bring in some cookies for you?"

No response.

I asked a few more questions, and nothing further happened.

With ghost children, I find that they are usually interested in playing with new ghost tools for only a few moments before moving on to the next thing. As a father myself, I understand how this works all too well. Luckily, I had a whole bag of tricks at my disposal. Next, I pulled out a strand of lights linked together that resemble oversized Christmas tree lights. These are fun to use because they change colors depending on how much electromagnetic energy the spirit uses on them. After placing them on the floor, I began coaxing Mary to touch them. To further help the cause, I placed a chocolate cookie in the middle of the lights.

After a few moments of waiting, one of the lights slightly blinked.

"Can you spike two lights this time?"

It took her a while, but she eventually complied and began spiking two lights every time she set them off. This in itself is amazing, since it shows that something with intelligence was interacting with me.

During this session, I really wanted to address some confusion I had about the little girl's name. I had found two different newspaper articles in the *Toledo Blade* that reported her death. One reported her name as Anna, while the other called her Mary (with her middle name being Ann). It was time to get the facts straight on the matter.

"Is your name Mary?"

Almost instantly, the light spiked. "Yes"

"Is your name Anna? Flash that light."

No response.

"So, your name is Mary?"

"Yes."

"Mary, are your parents here?"

During this moment, I caught an EVP of her saying, "No."

I continued. "I'm just afraid you're a little girl who's lost in the afterlife with no parents and you're just wandering around looking for mommy. I hope I got that wrong. Do you have your parents?"

"Yes."

Getting that response knocked me off my feet. Ever since I heard the stories of her roaming the theater and people capturing her saying the word *mommy*, it broke my heart, and I feared the worst. Confirming that she was indeed with her parents in the afterlife gave me faith that many of these ghost children are not lost after all but just having fun.

It would be hard to top that interaction but the Brown House wardrobe room was our next destination. While standing in the main room, I felt an odd, heavy thickness hanging in the air. The phenomenon I felt occurring here is something I tend to call a Frankenstein Tulpa. This is a process in which each object (or piece of cloth, in this instance) gives off its own unique energy that pools together and collects into one singular mashed-up energy form. This newly formed energy can then morph into a Frankenstein-like entity that is erratic and crazed, since it's been stitched together from so many sources. Sometimes, a collective energy like this can be manipulated by nasty forces or can gain a sort of consciousness. When it does this, it lashes out in dark ways because it is such a jumbled energy to begin with. This happens many times with houses built near cemeteries.

Later that evening, I returned to the Brown House to call out the energy responsible for scratching people. While putting my hand in a nearby closet, I felt a weird, cold energy shifting occur. Then with a digital recorder, I caught a very unusual garbled-sounding EVP. Upon reviewing the audio, it sounded like something said, "I like pain." Afterward, I performed a few house-cleansing rituals on the room, which I hope will put an end to the negative energy lurking in this space once and for all.

7

WSPD Radio Station

The building located at 125 S. Superior St. currently owned by iHeartRadio, may seem ordinary at first, but it's a location with a spirit that loves revealing itself when the right person comes along.

In 1907, the first radio broadcast out of Toledo took place in the Nicholas Building (608 Madison Avenue). In 1921, Toledo's first radio station, WTAL, was formed and then bought out in 1927 by George Storer. He changed the radio call letters to WSPD (which was an acronym of his business name, Storer's Speedene Gasoline), and he moved the station to the Commodore Perry Hotel in 1928, then 136 North Huron Street in 1940 and finally 125 S. Superior St. in 1955.

During the 1950's, the radio station had a popular afternoon show called *The WTOL Show*, featuring radio hosts Rudy Ertis and Joe Weaver. Ertis worked at the station for a long time before becoming the assistant manager in the '60s. In December 1969, Ertis was dealing with many personal relationship issues. He died by suicide after shooting himself in the station's garage on Christmas Eve. Many years after that tragic incident, a few of the station's radio disc jockeys began experiencing weird things around the station, including watching things being moved around and seeing shadows out of the corner of their eyes. Since they all knew Rudy had died by suicide there, they attributed anything paranormal to him.

Above: *Toledo Public Library.*

Left: A 1960s advertisement for the WTOL radio show featuring the host Rudy Ertis, who later died by suicide in the building. *Toledo Public Library.*

Once the older disc jockeys retired, they were replaced by new ones, which caused the activity to greatly calm down. According to popular AM radio host Fred Lefebvre, "I've been in this building for years and have never seen anything. The people who believe they saw something are all working elsewhere now."

Things remained that way until I came into the studio one day to talk about the paranormal.

MY ENCOUNTER

In the fall of 2015, I was lined up for an interview on the *Scott Sands* radio show. I arrived at the station to do some promotions for my first book, *Ghost Hunting 2.0*. At the time, I had no idea of the building's past. I was led down a long hallway and into the studio where Scott Sands records his daily show. Since he had a fascination with the paranormal, he wanted to talk about my experiences in Toledo. Before going live, he casually leaned over and told me that he used to hear stories of the WSPD building being haunted when he first started working there. He joked with me that I should ghost hunt their building sometime. When I pressed for more information on what happened, he said he heard a salesman had shot himself in the building's garage. Little did I realize at the time that this rumor was completely true. Scott Sands pointed to a large window on the far wall that peered into the control room on the other side of the glass. "We call that the ghost room." He went on to explain that a few odd things have happened in there. Again, I thought he was joking.

A few moments later, we went live on the air. The interview began, and he asked me all sorts of questions about my time at the Collingwood Arts Center as a ghost tour guide. About ten minutes into the interview, I was talking about the negative entity that likes to hide out in the center's basement, when suddenly, without warning, the live audio feed clicked out momentarily. As I kept talking, it happened again. I glanced over at the engineer sitting in the control room. She was frantically fussing around the control board, trying to figure out why the audio feed was dropping out.

Scott Sands ignored the technical difficulties and pressed on. After asking another question, a high-pitched screeching sound broke through over our audio feed. This was not normal at all. I looked back over at the engineer, who now had a panicked look on her face. She looked like a deer in headlights. The station cut to a commercial break, and two other radio guys ran into the control room. Scott even stood up to see what was going on in there. The engineer got on the microphone and said to us, "I've never had this happen before. I don't know what is causing it." I then turned to Scott and said, "Maybe it's your ghost!"

After coming back from the break, everything seemed to be fine. A few moments later, when I dove back into my paranormal stories, the audio feed started dropping out again. Every engineer at the station ran into the control room, all scrambling to fix the problem. Thankfully, my interview ended shortly after that. Scott turned to me afterward and said, "Sorry, I've never

The hallway of the WSPD studios in 1950. *Toledo Public Library*.

had that happen before." We silently exchanged glances because we knew what the real reason was without having to say it out loud.

A few years later, I emailed Scott about that interview for this book, and he remembered the experience all too well. He assured me that it was an isolated incident that he hasn't experienced since. I'm pretty sure Rudy still hangs around the station, waiting for the perfect opportunity to reveal his presence. I'm just honored that he chose me to make himself known to. If Rudy Ertis was trying to get my attention, mission accomplished.

8

DISCOVERY ACADEMY

The charter school at 2740 Central Avenue is by far one of the most haunted schools I've visited in the state of Ohio. After digging into the dark past surrounding this building, I quickly understood why this place is so haunted today. In fact, it might be a paranormal powder keg waiting to explode.

In 1920, the Toledo Society for Crippled Children opened and took in children with various polio-related disabilities. Public schools in the 1920s didn't accommodate children suffering from polio, so this school was the first to provide this kind of care. In the 1960s, polio was finally on the decline, so the school was sold to St. Anthony's Villa in 1963. The building then became a rehabilitation center for troubled teens who came directly from Lucas County's juvenal detention courts. During the 1990s, things began taking a dark and ominous turn, as tactics used by the staff turned barbaric. A former staff member revealed to me that psychological torture tactics were used on some of the more unruly teens in order to keep them in line. Lucas County also began sending over so many kids that the facility faced overcrowding issues. Many kids were placed in the same room, causing even more problems. Rumors have even surfaced about the large trash incinerator in the basement; it's said it was one of the ways kids were disappeared by the school. We may never know the full truth of what happened at St. Anthony's Villa, but it's well documented that Ohio's Family Services had to step in in September 2000 because law enforcement publically stated the school "violated children's rights, were

Chris Bores.

abused by staff, and failed to follow state codes regarding general safety, disciplinary policy and procedure." The school's license was revoked, and staff members were jailed.

In 2016, Discovery Academy purchased the building and turned it into a K–8 charter school. Even though everything within the building has returned to business as usual, the events of the past have seemingly started to bubble to the surface in a paranormal way. Recently, over a few years, I found that almost everyone working there has had at least one personal paranormal encounter. This is pretty alarming to report. I cannot provide any names in this chapter, but I will relay all their amazing stories.

Activity occurs frequently in the building and includes unexplained noises, sounds of children talking and laughing, voices, footsteps, shadow figures and strange feelings of being watched.

One teacher had something strange happen late at night during the school's annual Family Night event for children and their parents. After everyone left, she stayed behind to clean up her room. On her desk sat a pair of walkie-talkies that all the teachers used to stay in contact with each other during the event. As she was busy cleaning, she heard a little girl's voice break over the walkie-talkie static.

"Can you help me?" the voice asked.

The teacher was a bit terrified. She knew she was the only person in the school because the parking lot was empty. She immediately left for home and vowed to never stay after sunset again. A month later, the same thing happened to another teacher in a different part of the building. Again, it was a little girl's voice that crackled over the radio static, asking for help.

Another former teacher who's pretty sensitive to environmental energies had to quit her job because every time she went to work, she soaked up all the negative energy and came home depressed. She even started yelling at her family for no reason. Once she quit her job, everything returned to normal.

An upper-grade teacher experienced her classroom door closing all the time without explanation. She had to prop it open because an unseen hand kept closing it.

The school's former first-grade teacher was working late one evening and heard a group of kids laughing in the hallway when the school was empty. A few minutes later, she walked to the other side of the building to make copies in the school's office. Suddenly, she heard kids laughing again. She turned around and saw no one there.

The first floor experiences a lot of activity, but the second floor is said to be even more haunted. Every teacher working up there feels random cold spots forming and hears unexplainable noises throughout the day. One

The Toledo Society for Crippled Children in the 1930s. *Toledo Public Library*.

teacher even experiences her classroom lights shutting off all the time. She also hears unexplained footsteps in the hallway after school hours.

Another teacher on the second floor leads a classroom full of autistic students. Many times, she has witnessed all her students staring at something unseen in the room in unison. One time, specifically, a student of hers kept telling her that he saw a man in the hallway. When she peered out the door, she saw no one there. On other occasions, she has witnessed students pointing to a certain spot around the room with terrified looks on their faces. Another time, she watched as the entire class looked up at the ceiling in unison at just stared at something she couldn't see.

Even the school's custodian experiences things all over the building that he can't explain. He constantly feels like he's being watched. The school also has basement that is used for extra storage space. The custodian always feels uneasy down there whenever he's asked to fetch an item.

My Investigation

After hearing so many stories about this school, I knew I had to visit Discovery Academy for myself. Thankfully, I was given permission to poke around during the off season to see what I could find.

I began by roaming the hallways. The deeper parts of the building are devoid of any windows that give off natural sunlight, keeping them shrouded in constant darkness. I spent quite some time traveling through the dark corridors, going in and out of various classrooms with my meters. It wasn't until I reached the center of the school that both myself and the teacher who was showing me around heard a faint voice behind us. It sounded like a "Hey." We turned around and saw no one there. All that greeted us was a door leading to the basement.

I opened the door and headed into the dark abyss. As soon as I got to the bottom step, I felt a tense emotion. This was where I was told the most troubled teens were placed. I could only imagine what the staff did to them down here. I quickly found the room with the large incinerator sitting in the corner and felt something ominous in the air lingering around it. I couldn't put my finger on what exactly caused it. I investigated heavily in that area, hoping to get any meter spikes to happen. I turned up nothing. I did, however, feel like we were being watched. It felt like something was going to pop out at us at any moment.

In the basement of Discovery Academy, Chris interacts with the spirit of a young girl momentarily. *Chris Bores*.

We then made our way to the other side of the basement, which was directly underneath the kindergarten room. The air was much lighter here. I found a lone desk sitting in the hallway and decided to use it to set my ghost hunting devices on.

"Can you touch the meters on the desk there?" I asked. "They'll go off, and we'll know that you are here. Then we can talk to you."

The Ovilus ghost device I brought then spit out a word: *light*.

"Yep, this is a light all right. All you have to do is touch it."

I waited for a response. None came.

"Do you know the little girl that roams this place? We're trying to find her and say hello."

Seconds later, my K2 meter flickered slightly.

At that exact moment, I caught an EVP of what sounded like a young girl whispering, "Hi." This was amazing, since seconds earlier, I said I was hoping to find the girl and say hello to her. Was this her way of saying hello back to us?

I walked away from that area to explore the other side of the basement, but I decided to leave a camera behind to record anything that happened in my absence. About thirty-seven minutes into the recording, something really strange happens. The video feed starts flickering and then you can hear the night vision button being pushed off, causing it to record nothing but darkness. The camera feed flickers a few more times and then finally turns off. When I returned to the site later, I found the battery completely drained of its charge. There was no way this occurred naturally.

Exploring the basement was both thrilling and chilling. It seems that ghost students are roaming every inch of the building but are leery of strangers. I'd love to be able to return one day to help any spirits from the past that feel like they are trapped there.

9
FORSYTHE HOUSE

In 2014, the paranormal show *Dead Files* aired an episode in its fifth season titled "Demon War" in Toledo. This episode featured a demonically infested house at 917 Forsythe Street, which was built in 1910. The *Dead Files* crew was called out because everyone in the home, including Leslie Mullins, Angie Whitty, a daughter and a grandson, was experiencing dark paranormal activity. They heard strange noises, unexplained singing and knocking sounds; they were pushed and shoved; and things disappeared and moved around the home. They also saw a few ghostly apparitions. Downstairs, they saw a gray-haired man in a suit. In the stairwell, they've seen an apparition of a little boy. Leslie Mullins explained, "He had a burned face, burned arms. He appeared to have been in a fire."

The activity upstairs was a bit more sinister, as windows became unlocked and opened by themselves. What's even more troubling is that an apparition of a demon has been seen hanging around this area. "He didn't look human. He had two horns off the top of his head, big teeth, six foot tall and he came at me and went right through me. I immediately broke out in tears. I felt like I was going to faint."

Psychic Amy Allen from the show arrived with fifteen *Dead Files* crew members in tow. She instantly picked up on the long-lost tragic history involving an explosion that had happened down the street in 1898. In those days, grain elevators were built along the shoreline of the Maumee River. Close to the Forsythe House was the Union Railroad's grain elevator on Navarre Street. One day, it received a large shipment of grain, which caused tiny dust particles to oversaturate the air. The building's furnace filter was

Chris Bores.

damaged, and the grain particles ignited, causing the entire building to blow up. The *Toledo Blade* reported, "Everything within a two-hundred-foot radius was consumed in flames, broke out windows and melted railroad cars." One woman was even blown out a door and rolled down a hillside. Fifteen people died that night; three of them were kids.

Amy Allen walked around outside and sensed that many of the explosion victims were still wandering around the streets in pain and agony. She then walked into the house to see the little boy spirit. Amy knew he also came from that explosion incident, since he was covered with burns.

Allen then connected with the male spirit in the home. It turns out that he was a previous tenant from the 1900s named Clarence Brown. He had been trying to keep the family from being harmed by the evil entities upstairs. Once she heard that, Allen went upstairs to confront the demon. She came face to face with them and said there was more than one. Allen got the impression that they were never alive to begin with since they all had distinct bat faces. "They are here to take souls. Their goal is to possess [the grandson] so that they can function through him to do harm."

The aftermath of the grain elevator explosion in 1898. *Toledo Public Library*.

Amy Allen from the *Dead Files* sketched out this picture of a few demons she saw hanging around the bedroom. *Discovery Inc*.

She also sensed that the house itself wasn't haunted, but the people living in it were. They had done something in the past like play with an Oujia board that opened a portal for the demons to come through.

After locating the problem, the *Dead Files* team left the house and never provided a remedy to the family's problem. In typical paranormal TV fashion, they showed up, stirred things up and left without offering any assistance to the homeowners. This is one of the things I absolutely hate about these programs; they always seem more concerned about their ratings than helping the people in need. Just identifying the problem doesn't help at all; it only exacerbates the problem. And that's exactly what happened. The banging sounds became louder and more frequent, and activity occurred nightly for two months straight. It wasn't until the family sought out an exorcist that the house was properly cleansed. The demonic menace was finally purged.

Now, if you are looking to stake out the Forsythe House to experience the paranormal for yourself, don't waste your time. The family living there currently reports that all the paranormal activity must've followed the previous tenants to their new house, as they haven't ever experienced anything out of the ordinary. Since Amy Allen stated that she felt the family themselves were the cause of the haunting rather than the home, it would seem that is statement is proven true.

10

TOLEDO YACHT CLUB

When it comes to the Toledo Yacht Club, located at 3900 North Summit Street, it took me quite a while to uncover the complete past of this building, because it shares a history with another location that's been long forgotten in Toledo. In order to fully explore the haunted history of the yacht club, we have to start by taking a small detour north along Summit Street to a location where one of the town's most visited attractions once stood.

This area used to be known as Lake Erie Park in the late 1800s. (Today, it's known as Bay View Park). In 1895, the Casino and Scenic Railway Park opened with a row of attractions along the shoreline, including concession stands, a bowling alley, a nickelodeon, a shooting gallery, a dance hall, a carrousel and more. A long boardwalk stretched 1,200 feet over Lake Erie, connecting to the casino building, which was built on a wooden high rise over the water. The entire structure contained the casino and an auditorium/theater in the middle with 3,500 seats. It had an ice cream parlor/beer hall on one side and a restaurant on the other. Running parallel to the boardwalk was Toledo's first wooden rollercoaster that took riders out over the water. The site was so popular that a dedicated trolley line was built to connect downtown Toledo to Lake Erie Park.

When it comes to the Toledo Yacht Club's history, the organization itself was founded in 1865. The first clubhouse was erected in 1878 on a small island just over the Michigan border. It moved to the Neptune Building downtown in 1896 and then built a clubhouse at Lake Erie Park near

Top: *Toledo Public Library*.

Bottom: In 1900, the Casino and Railway Park was located down the road from where the yacht club would eventually be built. A long boardwalk stretched out over the water to connect the shoreline to the casino. *Toledo Public Library*.

Opposite: The new look of the casino in 1908, before a fire broke out, killing over five hundred people. *Toledo Public Library*.

Railway Park in 1898 because it brought many yacht-owning businessmen to the area.

Once construction was completed in 1908, Lake Erie Park was the place to be. The yacht club and the Railway Park held many joint events, including airshows, boxing matches and dances at the dance pavilion. Unfortunately, the casino was constructed using wood and was constantly plagued by fires. The casino building caught fire in 1900, then again in 1901, causing its owners to rebuild. The last and most destructive fire broke out on June 26, 1910, during an auditorium event around 11:35 p.m. As it quickly spread, the crowd of people rushed toward the exits, causing many to get trampled. A total of 519 people were killed in the chaos that night, as flames engulfed the entire structure. Even the casino's owner died in the disaster. Sadly, Railway Park was never rebuilt, and Lake Erie Park was never the same.

The Toledo Yacht Club became the lone survivor of that decade and went on to thrive. Over the years, however, the building quietly collected a few ghosts that couldn't let go of the past. The basement bar area is said to be very haunted. A bartender who was working late one night heard someone order a Manhattan cocktail. When she turned around to address the man, she saw the bar was empty. She believes the voice was that of a previous commodore who frequented there. Other employees have also heard his voice.

When it comes to the hauntings on the first floor, employees hear phantom footsteps walking around and see shadow figures around the room. The second level contains the club's ballroom with a women's powder room in

An aerial show during a joint event put on by the Yacht Club and Railway Park. *Toledo Public Library.*

the corner. People have reported hearing toilets flush by themselves and once saw a bluish shadow mist hovering a few moments before fading out. Event coordinator Susan Hurst once felt an unseen hand reach out and touch her in the back stairwell. Other staff members have reported experiencing the same thing on multiple occasions.

On the third level, it's said a young boy named Jacob was playing on the staircase in 1910 when he accidentally fell and died. Since then, people have reported seeing shadow figures at the top of the staircase. Some workers have even seen an apparition of Jacob peeking over the wooden railing. A bartender once went into the attic and saw him peek out from behind the corner momentarily.

The most intriguing part of this haunting is that when Susan Hurst's son reached the age of ten, the ghost child Jacob kept appearing to her son so they could play together. In a weird twist, the two actually became friends, causing Jacob to appear in human form often for him.

In 2014, I was asked to come out and investigate the yacht club to see what I could find. My stature can sometimes be a bit intimidating to ghost children, so I didn't capture a lot. I just experienced a few momentary spikes on my K2 meter in the attic.

Two years later, in 2016, the TAPS team from *Ghost Hunters* did an episode on the yacht club for their eleventh season on the SYFY Channel. During their investigation, they also hit wall when trying to contact Jacob until they brought in Hurst's son to help them make contact. Together, they coaxed him out of hiding to spike their meters a few times. The rest of their night was just as quiet as mine was when I was there. Interestingly enough, they also managed to capture an EVP in the attic. It was a voice that said, "I'm not Jacob." This is pretty amazing, considering how many deaths besides Jacob's I was able to find which happened close by. From commodores to casino fire victims, the list of likely suspects ranges far and wide.

11
Restaurants and Bars

Firefly Lounge (20 St. Clair Street)

Even though the Firefly Lounge has only been around since 2021, the business sits on history-rich land. Records are pretty spotty when researching the land pre-1870s, but earliest indications point to a residential home being there until the 1850s, when it was replaced by a business. That building then unfortunately burned down during the great Summit Street fire of 1873. The building was rebuilt in 1885, with a drugstore on the first floor and an apartment above it (Nellie Kettering lived upstairs). In the early 1900s, the location became the Bostwick and Braun Steel Works office, then Kirkby Machinery in 1920 (a supplier of metal and wood), Saba and Saba in 1974, Shared Lives Art Studio in 2011 and finally the Firefly Lounge in 2021.

The building went through a huge restoration in 2021 to convert the building into the upscale restaurant and bar it is today. This deep restructuring must have stirred up the spirits of the past, because shortly thereafter, two female employees encountered a ghost in the basement.

Jenna and Alexa walked downstairs to grab supplies. As they looked around, they heard a voice call out to them, "Hello darling." After hearing the disembodied voice, they both turned to each other and asked, "What did you say?" They quickly realized what had just happened. Jenna was a bit braver in that moment and took a few steps deeper into the basement. "Who else is behind us?" she called out.

Chris Bores.

"It's just us." The voice called back.

Both girls freaked out and ran upstairs.

A few days later, their bartender went downstairs and saw an apparition of man with a burned face appear before her. After she went home that evening, the entity followed her home. She saw the same face manifest in her living room.

Three days later, manager Josh Causer had an encounter of his own after closing time. "I walked out of my office and finished counting money. I reached for the door, and as I was closing it, I saw a little ball of light zoom past me. I stepped back and had goose bumps all over. I shut the door and heard someone in the back room. I was the only one here!" Hearing a voice come from the backroom is pretty interesting, since it's the same room that leads to the basement.

Shortly thereafter, I was called in and given access to the basement. I placed an EDI meter on a nearby chair in the hopes of getting the spirit to interact.

"If there is anybody down here who wants to communicate with me, now's your chance. All you have to do is hit those meters right there."

A second later, I caught an EVP of what sounded like a man saying, "OK."

I continued. "If you're down here, can you hit that meter for me?"

The meter spiked on command.

The basement of the Firefly Lounge is where the staff has seen the face of a burned man a few times. *Chris Bores.*

Wow—only five seconds into the investigation, and I was able to get both an EVP and a meter spike right after telling the spirit to do so. It didn't get much better than that.

"Can you do that again? I just want to know we are talking to something."

The meter immediately spiked again.

"Did you used to live here?"

Yes.

"I know St. Clair Street had a bunch of houses when this city first started. Did you have a house on St. Clair Street?"

Yes.

"So, was it your voice the two girls heard the other night?"

Yes.

"Do you like playing tricks on the people here?"

Yes.

"Do you feel stuck at all?"

No.

"Do you need prayers?"

No.

"Is this where you like to hang out then, the basement?"

Yes.

"There is a rumor that there was a fire here a long time ago. Were you involved in that at all?"

Yes.

This was quite the intense interaction. I decided to bring in my medium friend Marie downstairs to see what she sensed. "I get the name of Keith. I don't know what that's all about, but I'm also getting something about a woman. She's connected to the restaurant. I kind of get a teacher vibe."

When it came to the burned man, I was curious to figure out how he fit into all this. I did find a man named Thomas Taylor who died there on May 16, 1910, but I'm not sure what the cause was. I also uncovered that this location suffered from many fires back during the early days of Toledo. The nearby Indiana House burned down in 1850, then the Summit Street fire happened in 1873, the Hall Block fire in 1882 and the Wheeler Opera House fire in 1893. I swear fire was written into the DNA of this location. I'm not sure which fire the male spirit died in, but I hope one day to follow up on that.

EL CAMINO'S (2500 WEST SYLVANIA AVENUE)

In 1927, the El Camino Building started off as a drugstore, then became Anderson's Heritage Restaurant in the 1960s, Timko's Soup and Such in the 1970s, Harry's Martini and Cigar Bar in the '90s and El Camino in 2005.

Paranormal experiences at this location have long been reported on the down low, as they are only discussed among a small handful of employees working there. As I talked to some of the longest-working staff members, I was told that most of the activity occurs in the basement. "We feel odd feelings in the basement. We also hear odd noises and sometimes voices." The staff feels it's a male ghost haunting them, which they've named Tony.

As I headed down into the basement, I brought along my spiritual medium friend Marie. Right away, we both felt a quirky energy. "I feel a male presence that is a bit aggressive in attitude. I definitely feel that it's an old spirit from a long time ago."

"Was it from the Timko's era?" I asked. I was curious, since that's when Chris Woodyard visited this location for her *Haunted Ohio* book series.

"No, it feels like it was before that."

He was most likely from the period when the location was a drugstore. As Marie walked deeper into the basement, she pointed to a storage room in the back–left hand corner beside the bar. "Back there. Ask the staff if they get anything happening back there. I'm getting bad vibes from that area. I

Above: *Toledo Public Library*.

Opposite, top: The basement of El Camino, where people have seen and heard odd things. *Chris Bores*.

Opposite, bottom: The back storeroom area is said to be the domain of this territorial spirit. He doesn't like anyone going back there. *Chris Bores*.

don't know what is going on back there, but I don't want to go in there. He doesn't like people going there either." She then refused to take another step toward it.

I, on the other hand, dove headfirst into the small room, hoping something would pop out at me. Alas, nothing happened. It was just a quiet stock room. We walked over to a hallway behind the bar that leads back to a set of restrooms. When we headed toward the men's room, she said, "Oh, he likes messing with people in here."

Marie then stood in front of the other women's restroom door. "But not in the women's restroom, only the men's. He's saying, 'I respect the ladies.' I get the feeling that he doesn't even haunt any of the women workers here either. He won't mess with females. He has too much respect for that. It's how he was raised."

As we turned to walk away from the bathroom area, both of us unexpectedly heard the sound of a sink faucet turning on in the men's restroom. "Is that running water?" Marie asked.

"Yeah," I heard it, too. I checked out the bathroom, but there was no running water anywhere. I was baffled as to what made that sound.

As we headed back to the main area, Marie felt that this spirit had a hard time sharing the building with the current owners since he once owned it. "He keeps saying, 'This is mine!' He's proud that it's still being used, but he wants it all to himself."

When I pressed her for a name, she said it wasn't Tony like the staff named him. Instead, she felt more like it was Nathan or Nathaniel with the last name of Bodrey.

Unfortunately, at this time, I haven't been able to recover much to confirm that. Even though experiencing paranormal activity at El Camino is quite rare, I do hope to one day to return and find out exactly who this mystery man is.

TONY PACKO'S (1902 FRONT STREET)

In 1902, the Tony Packo's building was separated into a row of three or four individual shops housing various businesses from restaurants to tin shops. In 1932, Tony Packo's began as a little storefront down the street at 1935 Consaul Street, serving up sandwiches and ice cream. It also sold a unique Hungarian hot dog menu item that unexpectedly took the neighborhood by storm since it was cheaper and more flavorful than the products of other hot dog venders. Tony Packo's became popular overnight, and it then moved to the end of the street in 1936 after purchasing the entire complex. It knocked down the dividing walls that previously separated all the business and added a stage for live bands to perform on.

In 1972, history was made when actor Burt Reynolds was in town shooting a movie and stopped into Tony Packo's for a bite to eat. The owner's daughter asked for an autograph, so Reynolds signed a hotdog bun for them. After going on display, the bun created a lot of buzz, so the owners decided to

Chris Bores.

The interior of Tony Packo's. *Chris Bores*.

get as many celebrities to sign hotdog buns for them as they could. Today, that unique feature has put them on the map, as the restaurant has amassed thousands of hotdog buns signed by presidents, actors, musicians and more. With so much history centralized in one location, it's not hard to believe that a few ghosts are also around to join them.

According to Tony Packo's gift shop manager Jim Beard, most of the activity seems to occur around the gift shop area in the back of the restaurant. "I have seen people out the corner of my eye walk through the door. I've come rushing back and see no one here." Another time, he was folding T-shirts and felt someone walk up behind him. He then turned around to see no one there. A previous employee also witnessed a glass item float off the shelf and hover in the air a moment before dropping to the floor. Beard has also heard unexplained footsteps walking around in the room above. Another employee even claimed to see a young girl playing down in the basement years ago.

In the past decade, Tony Packo's has had three local ghost hunting groups investigate the haunted claims of the restaurant. According to Jim, "I sat through those investigations. There was nothing much to speak of." After hearing this, I knew the ghosts of Tony Packo's were very selective about who they reached out to.

As I dove into the history of the building, I ran across a tragedy that occurred on April 4, 1918, during the time that Munding Sheet Metal Tin Shop operated out of the building. It turns out that owner Robert Munding

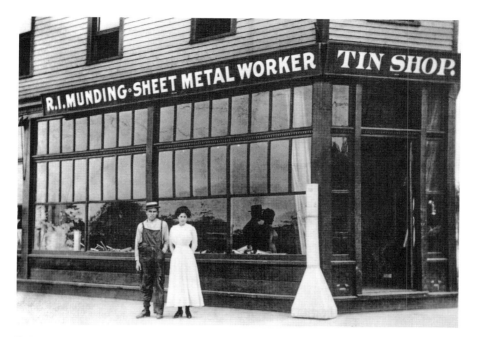

Robert Munding (pictured here with his wife) operated his sheet metal business out of the building Tony Packo's later occupied. Munding met a grisly end after getting into a fight with his wife's brother, who shot him six times. *Toledo Public Library*.

came home one night and beat his wife, causing her brother to get involved. Things escalated until the brother shot Robert eight times in the chest. The police investigated the incident and dropped all charges after determining it was done in self-defense.

With this shooting in mind, I brought my medium friend Marie in with me to see if she could sense Robert Munding anywhere in the building. As she walked around the gift shop, she said, "There is definitely something in here. It's not Robert though."

"Who is it?" I asked.

Marie stood there for a few seconds. Once the spirit heard us talking about him, he got excited and began flooding Marie with images. She was overpowered with the sensation. "I think someone got stabbed here!" Marie exclaimed. "Something with a sharp knife or a sharp object. He was stabbed and died here. He's excited that I can hear him. He's like, 'Here, please get my story out.'"

Unfortunately, we couldn't pull a name or date from the spirit, but I did find that a Joseph Beres died at that location on June 19, 1926. I'm not sure if that is the man in question, but he died at 1912 Front Street, the exact part of the building where the gift shop is located. Hopefully, I can one day go back and figure out exactly who this spirit is and provide him with the help he needs.

MANCY'S STEAKHOUSE (953 PHILLIPS AVENUE)

The current Mancy's building was originally built in 1907 and was first used as an Oldsmobile horse carriage dealership. After the business was sold in 1921, the building was split up into four sections: three downstairs and one upstairs. Gus Mancy had just emigrated from Greece and opened Mancy's Ideal Restaurant and Olde Tyme Saloon in the building. His eatery was successful out of the gate, and by 1970, he had purchased the entire building to expand Mancy's restaurant. As he began a series of upgrades in 1973, the sprinkler system was taken offline. Without a working system, a fire broke out and couldn't be contained. The entire complex burned down, causing $1 million in damages. The building was rebuilt and just recently celebrated its one hundredth year of service in 2021.

When it comes to the ghosts haunting this building, there are certain areas of the dining room in which employees have felt they were being

Chris Bores.

Left: Mancy's previous bar area with Tiffany lamps and an overhead stained-glass window from France, 1972. *Toledo Blade.*

Below: Firefighters battle a fire that broke out at Mancy's in the 1970s. *Toledo Public Library.*

watched or being followed around. Some have heard low whispering sounds coming from empty booths. One waitress even felt like she was touched by an unseen hand.

With these reports in mind, I visited Mancy's with Marie during its one hundredth anniversary celebration. As we walked around the front dining area, she instantly felt a male energy. "It's of an old man." She looked over at the wall to see the picture of founder Gus Mancy framed just inside the entrance's doorway. "That's him!" She stated. "That's who I'm feeling. I'm not sure if it's just him or more family members, but I feel a proud energy. The spirits know it's their one hundredth anniversary. When I walked in, they were like, 'Oh, we are so proud. This is our place!' The male energy is very happy."

This was an incredible thing to hear. I am glad to hear that Gus still watches over the restaurant he had to build twice to keep his legacy going strong.

MANOS GREEK RESTAURANT (1701 ADAMS STREET)

The Manos building was constructed in 1916 and used to be known as the Adams Bar throughout most of its early life. It's rumored that at one point, the upstairs area was used as a brothel. In 1981, Manos Paschalis purchased the building and opened Manos Greek Restaurant. Right away, ghostly experiences began occurring in the upstairs bar area. Activity occurred so often that during the mid-2010s, the local Fox news channel 36 did a segment on the haunted activity.

Chris Bores.

Workers often experience the most activity around the "Bass" mirror in the back corner of the bar. *Chris Bores*.

According to bar manager Amelia Jarrett, "We hear little things while we are closing when the music is off. When it's quiet, we hear sounds and see things out the corner of our eyes." Workers hear unexplained noises, like doors opening by themselves, voices from empty rooms and even footsteps walking around the bar when everyone is downstairs. A few bartenders have even seen an apparition appear around the "Bass" mirror in the corner of the room.

Owner Manos Paschalis explained, "My waitresses and cooks hear stuff all the time." He also said there is a rumor surrounding the upstairs area that a prostitute was once thrown out of the second-story window long ago.

I ended up heavily researching this location. I couldn't find any evidence to support the claim that a prostitute was thrown from a window, but I did uncover that the upstairs was previously an apartment before being converted into a bar. It turns out that a few months before Manos purchased the building, a previous tenant named Steve Szyskowski died upstairs on June 27, 1980, in the same area that was converted into a bar one year later. This was amazing to discover. It would seem that Steve is most likely the behind most the hauntings at Manos.

SIDELINES 2 SPORTS BAR/CAPTAIN WHIZBANGS (2111 MELLWOOD AVENUE)

The Sidelines Bar may have opened in 2005, but this location served as a BW3 from 1998 to 2004 and Captain Billy's Whizzbang Lighter than Air Fare from 1970 to 1994. This crazily named chain of seafood restaurants served many favorite seafood dishes from lobster to escargot. It had a full-service salad bar, frog legs and even had a gourmet seventeen-dollar peanut butter and jelly sandwich on the menu. Besides the haunting prices of peanut butter and jelly sandwiches, Captain Billy's is said to also harbor a few ghostly visitors.

I found a few previous employees who swear up and down that the place used to be haunted. They experienced weird noises late at night after closing, saw things move on their own and felt weird feelings they couldn't explain. Former employee Tobias Myers recalled, "The building is indeed haunted. I heard weird things and noises." He also experienced things in the attic, which was used for storage. "I went up once and just had an eerie feeling the whole time."

With these claims in mind, I visited the current sports bar to ask the current workers if anything was still haunting them. As it turns out, the bartender had some interesting encounters to reveal. "I've had TVs go off all by themselves. We've had the motion detectors go off when no one is

Captain Whizzbangs, 1980s. *Lois Coldiron and Gigi Jenkins.*

In the bar area, the bartenders will sometimes experience the TV's randomly turning off by themselves. *Chris Bores*.

An oddly placed tombstone sits on the side of the building. No one knows if the plot is real or not. *Chris Bores*.

in here at 3:00 a.m. Nothing was on camera, but the motion detectors go off saying someone is in here." The last thing she then mentioned was that the staff wondered if the activity had anything to do with a weird grave headstone on the left-hand side of the building.

"Wait, what?" I said, almost falling over. "There is a gravestone on the side of the building?" I literally heard a record skip as she said that.

I ran outside and plainly saw for myself a lone gravestone next to the building. I was shocked. Why was this even here? The bartender explained, "I think there used to be a headstone person doing business over here, so I don't know if it's a real grave or not." After doing some research, it turns out that she was right. Next to Captain Billy's sat Always Remember Granite and Monument Company that sold grave headstones. So, this is most likely not a real grave—but who knows for sure?

I brought my medium friend Marie with me, and she didn't feel anything around the gravesite. When she walked around the restaurant, she said, "I'm not getting anything here. I don't think any spirits are here per se. I think if there is, it's just passing through."

So, there it is, and this makes perfect sense. Any type of bar setting usually attracts wandering ghosts that have a taste for alcohol. They mostly like to feed off patrons with alcohol addictions. Many times, bars tend to have one corner of the room that feels darker than the others, and this is why. Thankfully, I didn't feel any dark corners in this place, so experiencing any type of paranormal activity at Sidelines would be rare.

Georgjz419 (1205 Adams Street)

Since 1877, this location has been used to house a variety of shops and church missionaries. Today, it serves as a nightclub bar called Georgjz419. George Thompson opened the bar in 2016 and experienced paranormal activity from day one as he began gutting the place. "I was working in the restroom, and I heard a plywood board slam down. I thought someone was in here. I yelled, 'I know someone is in here! I already called the cops!'" He looked around, but the building was empty. As the remodel continued, tools kept disappearing and reappearing in the oddest of locations. Once Thompson began hearing unexplained noises and voices he couldn't explain, he knew a ghost was behind it all.

One evening, Christmas lights were hung from the ceiling, and he noticed one of the bulbs was swaying back and forth all by itself, as if someone was tugging on it. Shortly after that, the staff experienced strange knocks at night, stones being thrown across the bar after closing, shadow figures in the kitchen and footsteps coming from upstairs. One time, a security camera even caught the image of a toy truck rolling around by itself in the basement. Thompson went down to investigate but couldn't find the toy truck anywhere.

The most interesting paranormal incident of all occurred on January 5, 2018, after the club had closed for the night. In a clip that lasts about fifteen minutes, the overhead lighting fixtures can be seen shutting off for no reason and then blinking wildly in random Morse code–type intervals. A few seconds later, the light beside it also starts flashing in the same manner. The staff was stunned. Georgjz419 called in local ghost hunter Chris Tillman to investigate, and his team was able to pull a name from the entity using their SB-7 radio device. They got the name Cooper twice in succession. After doing some digging on the building's history, it turns out that during the 1970s, the upstairs area was rented out by World War II veteran Orville Cooper. He died in 1978, and it seems he now haunts the building.

Not only is Orville Cooper a prankster, but he also helped out during a robbery one evening. The building alarm kept going off all by itself, causing Thompson to come back in and shut it off. It wasn't until he noticed someone hiding in the back room that the spirit stopped setting the alarm off.

With all the crazy things happening here, I decided to stop in with Marie. She instantly picked up on a male energy. "There's something definitely here. It's like an aggressive male energy beating on their chest saying 'I'm better than you are.' It's a fighting type of energy."

This is interesting because many nightclubs attract all sorts of parasite energies because of the alcohol. Whenever people with addictions gather in these areas, ghostly parasites tend to wander in with them.

When it came to the ghost of Orville Cooper, Marie couldn't find him. "I don't feel him in here. I don't know where he is." After talking with the owner, Thompson revealed that Cooper left at the beginning of the COVID-19 lockdowns in 2020. Since then, his spirit has remained very quiet, but he hopes that Cooper does return one day.

12

FRANKLIN PARK MALL AND OTHER RETAILERS

FRANKLIN PARK MALL

When it comes to the Franklin Park Mall, I was as surprised to find out that certain areas of it are haunted. Before the mall opened on Monroe Street in 1971, a small portion of its land was part of the Franklin Airport (from 1939 to 1952) and the Franklin Gardens, which contained a very small cemetery owned by the Sisters of the Poor. Now, you could blame all the hauntings in this area on the mall being built over this small cemetery, but it turns out, there is even more death attached to this land.

During the mall's construction, the main feature of the building was a huge cubical skylight in the middle of the mall that lit up and played music. It turns out that the guy who created it died before it was completed. As Nancy Robinson explains, "The architect who designed the cube skylight, Rich Osstiffin, was killed in a motorcycle accident just before the mall opened." The location of the cube rested high above the mall's original food court area, around where the current mall offices are located. A few employees who worked there during the mall's early years felt uneasy around that area late at night. Former employee Tess Westcott recalled, "I worked there for a couple of years. The food court at night was always kind of off-putting when I had to go to the office. The hair on my arms stood up, and I got goose bumps out of nowhere. I just felt like I was being watched." Could this have been the ghost of Rich Osstiffin still watching over his cube creation?

Toledo Public Library.

When I questioned a mall security guard about whether they had ever heard about anything paranormal happening at night, I was told he rarely gets a call for things like that, but it has happened. Very rarely, an employee will hear a door close by itself or a voice after closing that they can't explain.

While researching the history of the mall, I found one tragic incident that occurred in JCPenney on November 22, 1975. The store's first maintenance manager, Paul Gaul, suffered a heart attack on the sales floor. He collapsed and died there. Since then, a few employees swear the place is haunted. The haunting seems to be located on the second floor, around the employee's warehouse bathroom. Workers have gone to the bathroom and heard someone in the stall next to them when they knew they are the only person in there.

J. Alexander's (4315 Talmadge Road)

Believe it or not, the land owned by J. Alexander's is also reported to be haunted. This is most likely from when the building was the Walker-Feilbach Funeral Home, built in the 1930s. Talk to anyone who visited the funeral home back then, and they will have some interesting stories to share. William Getz recalled, "I used to deliver the *Toledo Blade* to that funeral home. I had to walk through the casket showroom in the dark to get to the upstairs apartment doors. It was quite spooky in there."

After the building became J. Alexander's during the 1990s, many servers began experiencing strange activity. Tobias Myers recalled, "I was a server at J. Alexander's for four years, and I witnessed some strange things. Liquor bottles would fall off the shelf and crash every few months." One of the stranger things used to happen after closing. "I used to crawl up in the rafters to change the lights. I swear I thought the cleaning people came in. I saw them walk in, but I would look around, and I would be the only one there!"

After doing some research, I found that a couple previously living there named Otto and Louise Kopitke, died in 1954 at this location. It's hard to tell if they still haunt the building but after visiting the restaurant recently, I was told that paranormal activity has ceased the last couple years. It seems whatever was there has moved on.

Toys "R" Us (5025 Monroe Street)

Before the building became Burlington Coat Factory, this Toys "R" Us building was definitely haunted. Former Toys "R" Us employee Carol Hagar worked as a night shift stock person and often heard strange noises and things being moved around all through the

Toledo Public Library.

night. "I did night shift, restocking toys. I would get done with an aisle, go to the next aisle, and I could hear the shelf being emptied. I'd run back over, and it looked like someone took their arm and pushed everything off the shelf."

I'm not sure why this location is haunted, since it was previously the site of a mini golf course. It's possible that either the funeral home ghosts or mall ghosts are wandering over to haunt this former toy store. Unfortunately after talking to current employees if things were still haunted, it sounds like whatever was there has left for good.

Sunforest Orthopedics (3900 Sunforest Court)

This business, which opened in 2006, may not be right next to the mall, but it's close enough. The staff regularly experiences the paranormal, and it turns out the reason might be because many of their patients die by suicide.

This facility sees a large amount of patients suffering from physical and emotion pains. When the pain is too great, some patients feel it necessary to take extreme measures and die by suicide. According to Amy Parker-Gardner, "My coworker and I had an experience at our office just before 6:00 a.m. A hand sanitizer can flew from the holder on the wall about four feet across an empty exam room and hit the door. There was some force behind when it hit. When the maintenance man came in later that morning, I asked him if the building was haunted. He said he had heard of other encounters." The staff has also experienced odd noises, lights flicking off and on and things disappearing and reappearing randomly.

FAMILY DOLLAR/FOOD TOWN (1703 AIRPORT HIGHWAY)

On the other side of town, you'll find one of the most haunted Family Dollars around. The reason for this is that before this building was built, the land was used for the St. Peter's Cemetery, which opened in 1867. In the 1920s, the city decided to use the area for commercial space, and it moved the bodies to the Calvary Cemetery down the street in 1930. Some bodies even went unclaimed, since their tombstones couldn't be read anymore. Those bodies were dumped in a single grave labeled "Calvary's Section 1."

National Foods then built a grocery store on the former cemetery grounds who then opened Food Town in the '60s. Employees began experiencing strange activity as soon as the store opened. According to former employee James Benner, "I was the nighttime head stock manager when it was a Food Town. It gave the cliche 'graveyard shift' credence. That building is truly haunted!"

Brian Morawski also recalled, "There was a lot of unexplained activity in that store at night when the night stock crew was working. It was always creepy as hell."

Tim Sigworth added, "I worked there on nights. We heard several strange noises in that building."

Food Town, 1937. *Toledo Public Library*.

After becoming a Sav-A-Lot/Family Dollar in 2003, the hauntings continued. Employee Wanda Davis recalled, "When the register was over by where the coolers are now, they used to have feminine pads. From time to time, they would just fly off the wall. The first time it happened, it scared the crap out of me!"

The store is so haunted that even shoppers witness activity. Toledo Kizwiz shared, "One time, I was in there, and the lights were flashing off. I was like, 'Oh, what is that?' The lady said, 'This place is haunted. The lights do that all the time.'"

RITE AID (4869 SUMMIT STREET)

Chris Bores.

When the staff at Rite Aid told me their building was haunted, I couldn't believe it. Everyone speculates that the ghost haunting this building originated from the Barge Inn business that was located there in the 1960s. It was a bowling alley/liquor store that lasted for quite a few decades.

Employee Chris Fall explained, "We definitely have a ghost. We see movement or shadows out of the corner of our eyes. Automatic doors open when no one is near them. The theft alert goes off with no one near it."

Things happen so often that employees have named the ghost John. According to Robyn, an employee, "We've had things fall off the shelf when no one is in the store. Stuff falls in the backroom when no one is in there. We even get cold bursts in the break room when we eat. But whenever we tell him to stop, he does it. It's really weird! We don't feel threatened or anything though." The activity seems to pick up after the sun goes down. "We get our floors done once a year, so somebody has to stay overnight. My supervisor was sitting out in the vestibule and saw a full-blown light orb float by in aisle 28."

Kaitlin Hoffmann, an employee, also added, "When I was closing with another coworker till 2:00 a.m., we stocked up boxes really nice in our elevator. We then left to go stock things, and the whole thing fell over. Everything got knocked down. We both didn't want to check it because we were so freaked out!" Hoffmann thinks John grew angry because the staff always leave the store by midnight. On that particular night, they were there much later.

With so much random activity occurring at this Rite Aid, I decided to pay a little visit with my medium friend Marie. She instantly felt a male presence. "Oh, he's a prankster! He loves to play jokes on the staff and get their reactions." Unfortunately, she wasn't able to sense anything else about him except that he was a good-natured spirit, wishing them no harm.

13

HISTORIC DOWNTOWN

COMMODORE PERRY HOTEL (505 JEFFERSON AVENUE)

This hotel was once one of Ohio's most luxurious, catering to Toledo's upper class. The five-hundred-room 19-story building opened in 1927, with building costs reaching $3 million. The main floor contained a lavish lobby, ballroom, restaurant and kitchen.

The second floor featured a Western Union telegraph office, a meat storage warehouse, a bakeshop, a coffee shop, personal dining rooms and a hospital. The original plans called for the building to have three separate high rises, but only two were built due to costs. Having separate towers provided natural light for every room.

The Commodore Perry Hotel attracted many celebrities, like Bob Hope, Elvis Presley, Jimmy Stewart, et cetera. It was even a popular location that many United States presidents throughout the 1900s opted to stay in while visiting Toledo. This included Harry Truman and almost every sitting president after him until Ronald and Nancy Reagan visited in 1980.

The hotel was losing money throughout the 1970s even though it had the popular Oliver's restaurant, Quarterdeck Bar and Motor Inn Fine Dining restaurant on the ground floor. Even the ballroom was rented out regularly for parties for premium rates. The Commodore remained open until 1980 and sat vacant for years before it was converted into an apartment complex in 1997. After the massive remodel, multiple workers and tenants alike experienced ghostly activity ramping up.

The Commodore Perry Hotel in 1970. *Toledo Blade.*

On the first floor, people have seen the apparition of a young girl. Some have even seen her roaming around the ballroom and restaurant and on the front steps crying. Other reports of activity include ghostly piano music playing from the ballroom when no one is in there. Today, the entire second floor is closed off to the public, but it's said the young girl haunts that floor, too.

The rest of the seventeen floors are used for apartments. They also have their own ghost stories attached to them. According to local astrologer Janet Amid, "When I do functions there, I feel the spirits, and I see orbs. I also smell scents from the past. One time, I was going up the elevator for a party. It was not clicking on the floor I needed. I stepped out of the elevator, and I felt that strong feeling like something was there. It just had that dark electrical energy."

Speaking of the elevators, another resident once saw a ghostly elevator operator from the past appear on one. According to Amid, "My client stepped on the elevator and saw an elevator girl standing there. She went up to her floor, got off and looked back. The lady had disappeared! It freaked her out."

Other tenants of the building are said to be haunted by shadow figures and strange noises. One person even saw a little girl in a white dress walk into a wall and disappear. Things seem to be most active on the fourteenth floor. According to Sammy Toledo, "Someone died in their sleep on the fourteenth floor about ten years ago. The body was there for a few days until management had to break open the door. A guy named Mario lived in the apartment afterward. He slept in the living room because an apparition haunted his bedroom."

Dan Walters also recalled the same haunting. "My brother Mario lived there from 2007 till 2020. He had weird crap happening all the time. He couldn't even sleep in his bedroom. Every time you tried to go to sleep, the room got cold, and there'd be a dark shadowy figure leaning over his bed."

An explosion destroyed the entire city block next to the Commodore Perry. *Toledo Blade.*

Sammy also recalled activity occurring in the apartment next to Mario's. "A couple who lived in the unit next door said their lights would flicker all the time, as well as other strange things."

As I dug into the building's past to figure out why it could be haunted, I found a horrible tragedy that occurred on February 13, 1956. A few buildings down from the Commodore Perry, a worker at Hy-Grade Foods meatpacking plant walked into a meat cooler where a faulty gas line was leaking gas. He lit a cigarette, causing the entire block of buildings to blow up in a huge explosion. The Commodore Perry was so close to the blast that most of its windows facing that direction were completely blown out. Three men died in the explosion, including Paul Borcherding, James Libhart and Melvin Kegelman.

In addition to those names, it seems many others have also died at the hotel: Robert Cummings in 1902, Mary Summings in 1908, Elizabeth Prentice in 1923, Ella Ranson in 1933, Samual Robinson in 1940, Gertrude Stevens in 1944, Louis Rogers in 1945, Charles Lillibridge in 1954 and Harry Tamier in 1955, among others. I'm sure at least one of these spirits is behind these hotel hauntings.

HILLCREST ARMS HOTEL (1601 MADISON AVENUE)

The last of the lavish downtown hotels to be built at the turn of the century was the Hillcrest. This $2 million building contained nine floors, 245 rooms, a roof garden and a 150-car garage. The hotel was visited by popular authors, artists and even Amelia Earhart in 1933. The hotel languished until the 1990s, when it was used as a Christian drug and homeless rehabilitation center. In 1994, a fire broke out and closed the hotel for good. The building sat vacant until 1999 and was then converted into an apartment complex, just like the Commodore Perry. As soon as the massive $12 million remodel was underway, workers began feeling the Hillcrest ghosts crawling out of the woodwork to haunt them. Their security guard witnessed all sorts of weird activity. "I worked there doing security when they were selling all the old stuff out of the hotel. Believe me, it was haunted!"

Jose Sifuentes added, "My daughter and her husband lived on the sixth floor. She would see black shadows. When they would be in bed, she would see it in the hall. Another time, she was lying on the couch, and she heard a very loud bang in her kitchen." Other times, the daughter came home to find certain windows randomly opened when no one had been home all day.

Another couple, Kevin and Michelle, also lived in the Hillcrest. They experienced shadow figures darting around their apartment and weird noises and voices they couldn't explain.

Scott Sifuentes had a friend who lived in one of the haunted apartments. "If you slept at her place, it would feel like someone was breathing by your ear. When you woke up, it would look like a shadow was walking into the bathroom. It was creepy as hell!"

Hillcrest Hotel, 1930.
Toledo Public Library.

The land the Hillcrest Hotel was built on was once part of a cemetery. The cemetery and Territorial Road were both removed in 1846. *Chris Bores.*

Even local astrologer Janet Amid admitted not liking the energy of the building. "It feels very heavy to me. It's like I feel like there was a lot of sadness there."

Hearing those words from Amid is interesting, especially after I uncovered a few pieces of Hillcrest's hidden history—about what the land was used for before the hotel was built there. After conducting deep research at the library, I found evidence that the building was constructed on a small portion of land that was once a cemetery.

Back in the early days of Toledo, the city had cemeteries on either side of town. The east side had Forest Cemetery while the west side had the little-known Madison Cemetery, the existence of which has been lost to time. If you've never heard of this cemetery, don't worry. No one else from this era has either. This is because it was located off the long-forgotten Territorial Road that was removed in 1846. Finding any evidence of this old road and its cemetery was difficult, as one of the few manuscripts even mentioning it is the *Maumee Valley and Pioneers* book from 1880. It tells us that the long-forgotten Territorial Road was one of the few roads that led out of Toledo and ran downtown to a wooden bridge on Swan Lake.

I also found another reference to the cemetery in a *Toledo Blade* article dated December 7, 1900. It provided a map with the exact location of the old cemetery on Territorial Road, which is where Madison Avenue and Sixteenth Street currently intersects. Unfortunately, all of that was dug up and removed once the city began constructing the Miami and Erie Canal in 1845. At the same time, it expanded all its existing downtown roads outward. Territorial Road and the Madison Cemetery were most likely removed in 1847, since M.A. Scott's writings in 1846 make reference to the cemetery. Once the new roads were built, most of Territorial Road was destroyed.

With the Hillcrest positioned directly over of the old Madison Cemetery, it makes perfect sense why this building is still haunted today. It turns out that the Hillcrest is most likely haunted by Toledo's earliest settlers.

TOLEDO CLUB (235 FOURTEENTH STREET)

The Toledo Club itself first began in 1879, when a group of Toledo's most elite businessmen gathered for drinks in various taverns around town. They eventually built a dedicated clubhouse in 1891 (located on the corner of Madison Avenue and Huron Street.) They only offered 350 memberships to the most local elite businessmen, like Edward Drummond Libbey, John Willys, Michael Owens and eventual president William McKinley. In 1915, their needs outgrew the building, and it was sold in favor of a larger building at 235 Fourteenth Street. The new club included two reception rooms, two bars, a ballroom, card rooms, private dining rooms and a gymnasium that was added in 1924.

Today, the building is still private, and the staff is haunted by a few paranormal guests to this very day. One paranormal story involves a drunken businessman haunting the fourth floor. In 1930, this club member got a little too drunk, fell over the banister and plummeted to his death. Ever since, employees have reported seeing a male ghost appear in that area. They've also seen various shadow figures haunt the entire fourth floor as well.

Another club member, William Schomburg, suffered a heart attack in 1962. He collapsed and died in the parking lot.

Local astrologer Janet Amid also had a rare encounter with the club's former bathroom attendant. "During their Halloween 2020 event, I had to use the restroom. I went upstairs, and the lights were on in the bathroom. There was this woman standing there. She had a black little outfit and hat on. I said, 'Hi.' And she just looked at me. I went to the bathroom, washed my hands and she just kept looking at me. I went, 'Bye,' and left. I went

Toledo Club, 1970. *Toledo Public Library.*

downstairs, and I was talking to the guy that hired me, and he said, 'You having fun?' I said, 'Yeah, but you have some strange people working here. I was upstairs, and your people didn't talk to me.'"

He looked at Janet, perplexed, and told her the upstairs bathroom was being remodeled and was closed for repairs. After explaining who she saw, he grabbed a picture off the nearby wall. It was a group photograph of the staff from the 1930s. In a *The Shining* movie moment, Janet looked closely at the picture to see the woman she had just seen upstairs in this picture. "Janet, she was with us for thirty-seven years. She passed away forty years ago!"

It sounds like there are quite a few spirits haunting this building today. Who knows how many previous members still roam their halls.

Mansion View Inn (2035 Collingwood Boulevard)

This beautiful Victorian house located in the Old West End was built in 1887 by Charles Reynolds. The eighteen-room mansion changed hands many times, from Leroy Ludwig in 1894, to Jay Secor in 1904 and, finally, to the Stewarts in the 1930s. The Mansion View Inn was used as a strip motel during the '50s before finally being turned into a bed-and-breakfast in 1987.

After becoming a bed-and-breakfast, owner John DuVall reported to the *Toledo Blade* that he was constantly experiencing paranormal activity. Duvall experienced things like seeing an apparition of a woman and hearing faint laughter coming from the parlor room; he even saw a ghostly hand appear on top of the staircase post before disappearing.

When it comes to people staying at the inn, complaints always came from Room 301. Guests were woken up by whispering sounds and the feeling of something pressing down on the mattress.

Unfortunately, the Mansion View Inn is now closed to the public since it was sold to the Old West End Association in 2015.

Trilby Sullivan Farmhouse (5800 Atwell Road, Previously 3048 West Alexis Road)

In 1991, the *Toledo Blade* ran one of its first paranormal stories about a man who was experiencing activity in his home. It turns out that the

WADE BROTHERS GET A
FRESH LEASE OF LIFE.

Men Convicted of the Murder of Kate Sullivan,
and Sentenced to Die Today, are Given Another Chance for Their Lives by
the Supreme Court.

Top: The Trilby Farmhouse. *Toledo Public Library*.

Bottom: The murder of Kate Sullivan was major news throughout Toledo, especially when her murders were being convicted. This is a banner that appeared in a Toledo newspaper on November 21, 1903. *Toledo Public Library*.

1887 farmhouse he lived in was the exact location where one of the most famous murders of the last century occurred.

On April 14, 1900, fifty-five-year-old Kate Sullivan and her sister Johanna came home with a large sum of money because they had sold off a bunch of land and livestock. As they celebrated at home, two masked men broke into their house, looking for the money. They slammed Kate's face into the wall repeatedly and beat both women over the head with blunt objects. After tying both bloodied women up, the men tore up carpets, cut mattresses and finally found $200 hiding in a closet. Once the men left, both women got up and staggered off in opposite directions to reach neighbors houses for help. Kate collapsed in the process and died. The horrific news of this tragic event took the entire city by storm. It took police three years to finally capture the men responsible. They turned out to be local horse thieves, Al and Ben Wade. They were sent to the electric chair in 1904, after a long court battle. For decades after the incident, people from all over drove by the farmhouse to see the famous murder site for themselves.

By 1948, the history of the murder had become a forgotten memory. The house was sold to Richard Morrill, who split the home into a duplex rental property. It wasn't until the 1980s that house renter Julie Denniss began experiencing weird activity. One evening, she saw an apparition of an elderly woman in a long dress and boots. "She was standing in the dining room. She kept staring at me. I looked up, and she was gone." Was this the spirit of Kate revealing herself?

In 1991, renter Ron Musser also experienced strange events. "I used to go into the kitchen, and the silverware drawers would be hanging open. No one had been in there." He also heard unexplained noises and saw things he couldn't explain.

After the renters moved out, things seemed to quiet down. According to the current homeowner, Mike, "I haven't heard any stories from other people. We've been over there at midnight working on the house, and they've never bothered me." So, either Kate has found peace in the afterlife, or she's waiting for the right tenant to come along before making herself known again.

Fort Industry Square (150 Summit Street)

The oldest and most historic spot in downtown Toledo has to be the row of buildings on Summit Street called Fort Industry Square. This historic hot spot dates to the 1650s, when French troops from the Canadian Territory built a trading post there. The fort was so strong that it was still standing when soldiers utilized it as part of a larger military blockade against British troops in the early 1800s. Afterward, the fort was finally removed and replaced in the 1880s by a row of business buildings that were constructed over 144,000 square feet and still stand today.

When I talked to a few business owners about the haunting of Fort Industry Square, everyone pointed me to the left-hand side of the building. It seems

Fort Industry Square, 1897. *Toledo Public Library.*

Fort Industry Square, 1976. *Toledo Public Library*.

that 150 Summit Street is the most haunted area, where one rumor suggests that a woman was decapitated long ago in an elevator accident. According to Kelley Knitz, "I had my office in Fort Industry Square. I always heard doors opening and closing on their own."

Scott Myers feels that the fourth floor in particular is haunted. "I was alone in the vacant building one evening, and I felt like somebody was watching me. The hair stood up on the back of my neck, so I ran downstairs and out the front door. My brother told me a woman died up there in the early 1900s."

While digging into the history of the area, I couldn't find any evidence of a woman dying there, but I did run across a disastrous fire in 1898 that took down the Lorenz Building located directly behind it. This fire also took the life of a fireman who was trapped inside when the building collapsed. Since the Lorenz Building used to sit behind the 150 Summit Street building, it's a good bet that the fireman still haunts this location today.

14

LIBRARIES

TOLEDO DOWNTOWN LIBRARY (325 NORTH MICHIGAN STREET)

Before this location became Toledo's main library, Toledo's Central School occupied the land from 1853 until catching fire and burning down in 1895. After the Toledo library was built, staff and visitors alike seemed to encounter occasional bursts of paranormal activity happening there throughout the years. The main hot spot is said to be the second floor, where people have seen the apparition of a woman. It's also the area where many strange and unexplained footsteps are heard coming from the floor above (the third floor). This is interesting to note, as no one working on the third floor has ever experienced anything. According to one employee I talked to, "There's an old lady ghost that hangs out on the second floor. A bunch of people I worked with have experienced weird things there after closing time. Even when I was a kid in the '70s, the library was well known for this mysterious ghost lady."

The basement is also another hot spot for activity. The library staff has seen shadow figures, felt random cold spots and gotten unusual feelings of being watched in the backroom areas that are closed off to the public.

After talking to a few security guards, it turns out that even they will sometimes get weird camera anomalies of shadows in the hallways appearing almost human in form on their security camera footage late at night.

Main Library, 1940. *Toledo Public Library.*

While digging into why this library could be haunted, I was told a rumor that someone died during the building's construction when a crane fell over and killed one of the workers. Unfortunately, I couldn't find any evidence of that, but I did find the obituary of Clara Bourdo, who died across the street in 1891 at 324 North Michigan Street. Is her spirit the one haunting the library, or could it be a teacher spirit from when the land was used for Toledo's Central School? Until a thorough investigation is conducted, that answer remains a mystery.

WEST TOLEDO BRANCH LIBRARY (1320 WEST SYLVANIA AVENUE)

When it comes to the West Toledo branch, built in 1930, the location is ripe with ghostly rumors. It's said that a few librarians who worked late into the night have seen an apparition of a priest. This is pretty interesting, as many pieces of a church were included in the building's architecture. Other reports include the staff hearing odd noises and thumping sounds coming from the kid's area fireplace room after closing.

I decided to visit this library with my medium friend Marie to see if we could find anything. She wasn't able to find any trace of a priest haunting the building, but she did connect with a female spirit after heading into the

Left: West Toledo Library, 1920s. *Toledo Public Library*.

Right: The basement of the West Toledo Library is home to a female librarian. *Chris Bores*.

basement. "I get the feeling that this is a librarian from the old days. She loved kids and organizing the library events here. I think her name is Sandy or something like that with the last name starting with a B, like Berger or Borger. She's sad that the kids don't come here anymore. She wants the kids to come back."

I find it interesting that she misses the kids, because it's pretty evident that kids don't really visit the library as much they used to. In the end, Marie gave us one final message from our ghost librarian. "She wants people to know she's still here, and she loves the kids. She wants them to come by whenever they can."

BIRMINGHAM BRANCH LIBRARY (203 PAINE AVENUE)

When it comes to the paranormal at the Birmingham branch, built in 1925, things usually happen down in the basement. One recent event involved a doll that was locked away in a display case. One morning, librarian Julie McCann noticed that one of the dolls was turned completely around. This was troubling, since she was the only one with a key to unlock it. According to McCann, any ghostly activity that occurs there is usually attributed to the ghost of Catharine Gorman. She was the branch's very first librarian who died in 1958.

Other ghostly reports include workers hearing unexplained knocks after closing and people getting a heavy feeling once they reach the bottom step of the stairwell leading into the basement. McCann explains, "I heard someone fell down the stairs and may have died around thirty years ago."

One morning, librarian Julie McCann went downstairs to find that one of the dolls inside of this locked glass case had been completely turned around. No one had a key except for her. *Chris Bores*.

In 2010, the local ghost hunting team Fringe Paranormal conducted an overnight investigation there. While in the basement, they heard footsteps coming from above and a noise that sounded like a man clearing his throat.

With this in mind, I dropped by the library with Marie. As we walked down the steps to the basement, she instantly picked up on something when she reached the infamous bottom step. "I feel a very weird energy right here. I don't know what this is all about, but it's along this bottom step."

After wandering around the basement, she briefly connected with Catharine Gorman. "She's hiding. I don't think she wants to talk to strangers. She'd rather interact with people she's more familiar with. She's a bit shy but feels comfortable around Julie." Marie went on to explain that she sensed Catharine loved seeing the kids come to visit. "This is her comfortable place. She doesn't want to bother anybody or scare anybody intentionally, but she'll play a random joke here or there on the librarians. Nothing about it is malicious in any way though. She loved being here and now just wants to stick around."

As you can see, most spirits don't need to die tragically in an area in order to haunt it. They could be a former worker or visitor who is touring in the afterlife.

15

WOODLAWN CEMETERY

Now, you may ask yourself: What on earth could haunt a cemetery, especially one that has been a staple to the city since 1876? Well, a lot actually. In fact, cemeteries are usually home to many parasitic spirits that lurk about in the afterlife, especially ones trying to cope with the reality of being dead.

The most popular urban legend surrounding this cemetery involves a lady in white appearing in a long white dress around the front gate late at night. It's speculated that she hangs around searching for her long-lost daughter. Even the people who live in the houses behind the cemetery on Jackman Street have also reported seeing other apparitions of little girl ghosts. One person told me they once saw two girls playing by the fence in Victorian-style clothes. Jennifer Pegorch also saw something similar. "My sister and I lived on Burton Avenue. We saw a little girl in a white dress by the pond. It was an older-style dress, and she had curly blond hair."

Alex Sauceda once witnessed something very unusual. "My friends were in the cemetery at midnight, and there was a blue orb floating around, like, twelve feet in the air!"

Others, like Pat Williams, had a very different experience altogether. "We would hold séances to call up the spirits in the mausoleums. On a quiet night, I swear we could hear them!"

One person recalled a story that ran in the *Toledo Blade* during the 1960s involving two teenagers who cut through the cemetery on their way home. As they walked through a foggy area, they were maliciously scratched until

Chris Bores.

they reached the exit gate. When they got home, their parents called the police. The police officers then went to the cemetery and retraced the boy's footsteps. They, too, became scratched up as they entered and exited the same mysterious foggy area.

After talking with the locals, it seems the Woodlawn Cemetery isn't the only place in the area that is being haunted, as the people who live in nearby houses have experienced hauntings. According to Nancy Suber, "We lived across the street. We always had lots of things happen in our house."

Linda Holden added, "We lived at 3655 Burton Ave. for quite a few years. We experienced a lot of strange happenings." Activity ranged from unexplained sounds to ghostly shadows at both locations.

MY INVESTIGATION

One afternoon, I headed out to the Woodlawn Cemetery to record an introduction to my ghost video. I placed a fresh battery in my camera and proceeded to record my introduction sequence around section no. 28 of the cemetery. I spent ten minutes filming my scenes, threw my equipment in the car and headed for home. When I tried reviewing my footage later, I discovered my camera wouldn't power on. The battery was completely dead. Something had drained my battery.

Another ghostly encounter I had at the Woodlawn Cemetery took place in section no. 37. I was working with my Ovilus device. "Give me your name." I kept asking. I got no response. I walked back to my car and opened the door. "Can you give me your name? If you can't give us a name, I'm going to leave."

Suddenly, a word appeared: *property*.

"Property?" I closed the door and put my key in the ignition. "Sorry, that's not good enough. I wanted a name, and you didn't give us one, so we're leaving."

Almost instantly, two words appeared in succession: *paranormal* and *enemy*.

I looked down and burst into laughter. "So, that's what you think of me, eh?"

As you can tell, there are strange things afoot at the Woodlawn Cemetery. If you decided to visit, make sure you keep your camera batteries in a safe location, or else they will become food for the spirits.

16

SCHOOLS

UNIVERSITY OF TOLEDO

Founder Jesup Scott had the dream of building a university on a 160-acre piece of land he owned outside of town. The approval process from the city took years to complete and unfortunately, Scott died in 1874, ten years before the city granted his approval. Once approved for construction, the Jesup Scott Trust moved forward and built the University of Toledo.

Over the years, the university has become home to several paranormal hauntings. Many of them focus on one dormitory in particular: Carter Hall. It's said that in the first-floor bathroom, sink faucets and showers turn on by themselves. According to student Nancy Bartaldo, "One of the first-floor men's bathrooms has a ghost that turns water on in the showers. I turned it off, but then it turned right back on!" Another student heard someone washing their hands one evening, so they walked over to the sinks and saw no one there.

Even teachers have fallen victim to the college hauntings. "I was teaching, and the lights would go on and off at random points during my lecture," recalled Ammon Allred. "At first, I thought it was the motion sensors acting up, but that couldn't account fully for it, because once or twice, they just dimmed."

Stroll over to University Hall, and you'll find another hot spot of activity. According to Patricia Carmean, "I did not like to be on the top floor at night for my music classes." She always felt like she was being watched.

Toledo Public Library.

Linda Edelman added, "In the 1980s, we would be in the darkroom late at night. It always felt like we were being watched."

James Ong recalled another hot spot. "My friend and her ex-boyfriend snuck inside the field house before it got renovated." As they walked onto the basketball gym floor, they momentarily caught a glimpse of something in the darkness playing basketball before suddenly vanishing.

Over in Dowd Hall, there is a rumor that a female student was raped and murdered in the basement. Her restless spirit is said to haunt the area and frighten any male who dares enter.

Paranormal activity even seems to happen in the former Alpha Omicron Pi sorority house in the Greek Village. It's said to be haunted by a ghost named Stan from the Sigma Alpha Epsilon fraternity. Apparently, he died there in the early '90s.

Paul Anthony recalled that the Omega sorority house was also haunted. "I heard a story about a girl that was murdered there in the 1950s. We went to the house, and it actually felt cold over there. I didn't feel so comfortable, but I can assure you there is something there."

Even the university's Medical Center Hospital has some amazing activity. Former resident Amy Dorty explained, "I'm not sure of the floor, but the ER Department always reports seeing shadow people darting around. This includes the surrounding hallways. They always hear sounds of talking and whispers when no one else is around. Call lights go off by themselves when no one is in the rooms." Dorty even had a spooky encounter herself late one evening. "I was in the ER, and I witnessed a person walk through a wall where there used to be an office. It was very brief, and it just disappeared."

If you are wondering who could be haunting the university, well you'd be surprised at the list of names I turned up. I couldn't find information on anyone being murdered in Dowd Hall, but I did find one sorority house student, Michael Beier of Alpha Sigma Phi, who died in a 1966 swimming accident.

When it comes to school faculty, university president Dr. Ernest Smith died in 1926 of heart disease. The next university president, Dr. Henry Doermann, also died in 1932 of disease. (So, was there a curse on university presidents here or what?) Vice-president Lee MacKinnon died in 1935 from a heart attack. Professor of history Glenn Bradley died in 1930 of infection. Professor of biology John Condrin died in 1937 during surgery. Professor of political science Garfield Jones died of pneumonia in 1957. Professor of history Miss Janney died in 1967 from an illness. Professor of business Richard Lower died by suicide in 1973. Assistant dean Sherman Smith died in 1960 from an illness.

As for the students, Howard Barr died in 1950 in a nearby car accident. Frank Jason died in 1953 in his dorm room from a drug overdose. Douglas Milek died in a car crash in 1968. Anthony January collapsed and died on the football field during practice in 1973. Robert Morrison and Roger Carroll died in a car wreck in 1974. Basketball player David Roecker died in 1977 due to an illness. Four Indonesian students were killed in a car crash in 1989. Andrew Brown shot his girlfriend seven times and killed her in their dorm room in 2006. Josiah Galat was stabbed to death in the stairwell of the Horton International House in 2012. University police officer Jeffrey Hodge shot and killed Melissa Herstrum in Scott Park in 1992.

With so much death centralized in one place, it's no wonder this school has so many hauntings. This university is definitely in need of one deep spiritual cleansing.

WAITE HIGH SCHOOL (301 MORRISON DRIVE)

Waite is one of the oldest high schools in Toledo, as it opened in 1914. Oddly enough, this school has a ridiculous urban legend about the architect building the school backward and dying by suicide afterward. This is completely false

Toledo Public Library.

since the real architect, David Stine, didn't die by suicide. In fact, he went on to design other buildings in Toledo many years after.

One haunting that is plausible here involves a spirit the basement. It's said that a student drowned in the pool room years ago and still haunts it. According to Raymond Schilt Jr., "The pool room is legitimately haunted. I heard banging noises and voices down there when a friend and I were gathering extra textbooks for a teacher back in 1999. A few books fell off the shelf without being touched or us being near them."

When I researched if anyone died at the school to validate this claim, my research turned up a few records. The first death was that of football player Norman Wolford, who died on the football field while playing against Point Place High School in 1930. Student Paul Harris also died in 1945 while traveling to an away game.

However, the death of Maryann Fangman is probably the one that spawned the pool room haunting rumor. She died shortly after graduating in 1947, and the newspaper reported that her cause of death was from a "forty-foot plunge." Despite the odd choice of words for this headline, she didn't actually die in a pool-related accident. She died because she fell out of an amusement park ride, forty feet down into the water below, which killed her. Since the headline mentioned that a "forty-foot plunge" killed this student, it probably started this urban legend of her spirit haunting the pool room. Without doing a deep investigation of that area, we will never know if she actually does haunt the school.

JEFFERSON JUNIOR HIGH SCHOOL (5530 WHITMER DRIVE)

Jefferson Junior High School was constructed in 1924, with a huge bell inside a belfry tower on top of the school. The bell used to ring loudly throughout the neighborhood at the beginning of each school day. Decades later, before the bell was removed, it was said that it would sometimes toll by itself after midnight without anyone being in the building.

Chris Bores.

Everyone speculated that the person behind the hauntings of the school is a former janitor named Oscar. Kids have reported seeing Oscar's ghost around the school, especially in the theater room. He is usually seen in the upper balcony section looking down at the students below. If any brave student dares to head up to the balcony to look for him, do not sit in his favorite seat, or he will get angry and lash out. He also gets mad if kids wander up there and say they don't believe in him.

CENTRAL ACADEMY (3100 KING ROAD)

Central Academy once stood from 1929 to 2014 before it was demolished and replaced by the Mercy Health Medical Center in 2015. When it was a working school, teachers reported seeing shadow men in its hallways, hearing unexplained noises and even seeing shadow figures dart past windows late at night. One teacher constantly had things in her classroom go missing, so she resorted to making Xerox copies of everything so she always had backups.

While doing some digging into the history of this school, I found that a student was murdered there in 1968. Student Eileen Adams was abducted after school, and they found her beaten body a month later, rolled up in a carpet outside of town. Could Eileen be the one behind the school hauntings?

Even after the school was demolished in 2014, the medical center that replaced it also seems to be haunted by the same type of activity. Current employees keep reporting that they are still seeing shadow figures, hearing odd whispers, smelling mysterious smells, feeling cold spots and witnessing medical equipment turn on without anyone touching it.

DeVilbiss High School (3301 Upton Avenue)

DeVilbiss High School (which is now Toledo Technology Academy) was previously in service from 1931 to 1991, and the hauntings that plagued this building mostly occurred on the third floor. Activity occurred so frequently that the custodians refused to work up there alone. They often saw shadow figures and heard strange noises they couldn't explain.

As I researched the school's history, I found an unusually high number of car wrecks involving students from DeVilbiss. There were so many, I couldn't help but wonder if the word *devil* being in the school's name had something to do with it. Glen Higle died in 1934 when his car was hit by a train, Evelyn Snyder died in 1947 in a collision, Richard Messer died in a motorcycle crash in 1955, Keith Ryan died in 1956 in a collision and the list goes on.

Toledo Public Library.

Fall Meyer Elementary School (1800 Krieger Drive)

Fall Meyer once operated from 1951 to 2007. It's reported that the ghosts of former basketball players used to haunt this school's unused locker room. Many times, teachers heard the sounds of a basketball bouncing around when the room was empty. Other unexplainable sounds, like doors opening and closing by themselves, were also heard. Sadly the building has been long demolished so we will never know the truth behind the haunting.

Start High School (2010 Tremainsville Road)

Built in 1962, Start High School is haunted by poltergeists that loves making lots of noise. This ranges from unexplainable sounds to disembodied voices. Many of the rumors I was told mainly involve the art room. One former teacher told me they always had things in their classroom completely disappear and turn up later in weird locations. She also heard strange sounds coming from her storage room on a daily basis. Whenever she walked over to inspect it, the sounds would cease. This happened for months.

One night, she came face to face with the ghostly figure that was haunting her room. While working late one night, she happened to glance over at the far wall, which had a mirror on it. She saw a reflection of a shadow person standing next to her. When she turned to look at what it was, she saw nothing there.

Two other teachers have also seen shadows and heard unexplainable noises in the same classroom. One of them believes the spirit is the school's old art teacher who recently passed away. The other teacher believes it's something more sinister.

REACH ACADEMY (2014 CONSAUL STREET)

St. Stephens Catholic School, now called Reach Academy, was built in the 1930s next door to the St. Stephens Church. For years, teachers experienced encounters with a ghost that was hanging around the girl's bathroom on the main floor. Some teachers think that the ghost is the spirit of a nun who worked there, while others think it's the spirit of a student or a young girl. Activity happens so often that they've named their ghost Rosie. As one teacher explained, "We have little ghost kids that love haunting us around the building. Rosie likes to hang out around the bathroom area and turn on sink faucets and shut bathroom stall doors a lot."

Another teacher told me, "I didn't enjoy working there late at night because I would go to the bathroom and feel like I was being watched the whole time. I would also hear odd sounds I couldn't explain."

Chris Bores.

17

DEMOLISHED AND ABANDONED

RIVERVIEW INN/SUMMIT BAR AND GRILL (127 NORTH SUMMIT STREET)

The former site of the Riverview Inn has many paranormal rumors surrounding it, and they are mainly centered on the Summit Bar and Grill restaurant previously located on the nineteenth floor.

Before a hotel was built there, the location was home to the original downtown Sears building. By 1970, Sears had relocated, and the building was replaced with a Holiday Inn that cost a whopping $7 million to construct. The hotel became the Riverview Inn during the 1980s and then went through a tumultuous period in which it became the Toledo Tower in 1995, Best Western in 1997, Hawthorn Hotel and Suites in 1999, Ramada Inn and Suites in 2001 and finally the Hotel Seagate in 2004 before completely closing in 2009 due to burst water pipes that failed to pass Toledo's fire code inspection.

The haunted Summit Bar and Grill first opened in May 1999, during the hotel's Best Western days. From the start, staff began having weird experiences they couldn't explain. They felt like they were being touched, heard unexplained whispering sounds, and the morning crew often came to work to find items moved around from the night before.

Things came into focus one day when a worker saw an apparition of a woman in the Summit Bar and Grill late at night. From then on, they were able to put a face on most of the hauntings that occurred in the restaurant. For years, the entire hotel staff was made aware about the Riverview Inn's

The Holiday Inn/Riverside Inn Hotel. *Toledo Blade.*

hauntings through workplace gossip. Former security officer Allan Sandusky remembers, "I did security there, and I was told about a ghost woman on the top restaurant level. I never saw her though"

This ghostly encounter then morphed into a rumor about a woman who died by suicide after jumping out of her hotel window. I was trying looking for any documentation of this tragic event taking place there, but unfortunately, I couldn't find any.

Interestingly enough, the first business to open up on the nineteenth floor during the Holiday Inn tenure was a nightclub called the Marco Polo Room that opened in 1970. Having a nightclub with alcohol and people's hormones can attract all sorts of parasite spirits that love feeding off the living. Once the location was remodeled into a bar and grill, the parasites probably stuck around in hope of finding a new source of food.

The concept image of the Holiday Inn Hotel, 1971. *Toledo Blade.*

The pool area was said to be another haunted hot spot, since it was also on the top floor right next to the restaurant. Rumors stated that every so often, security cameras picked up random unexplained ripples in the pool's water. One person even claimed the Riverview Inn's promotional flyer from the 1980s showcased a hotel room picture with a strange orb floating around in it. When looking closely at the orb, one can see it has a ghostly woman's face inside of it.

Paranormal activity even occurred on the penthouse room floors. Guests would sometimes experience strange knocks on their door late at night. Once opening the door, they were greeted with an empty hallway.

As I searched for any deaths that may have occurred in that area, the only one I found was that of Frank McCarthy, who died in 1908. I'm not sure if he was the one behind the hauntings, but unfortunately, I couldn't find any evidence of a woman dying there, so I am still unaware of why her spirit remains there.

RIVERSIDE HOSPITAL (1609 NORTH SUMMIT STREET)

Rumors of the Riverside Hospital being haunted started long ago while the building sat vacant for years, all boarded up. This gave creepy vibes to anyone driving by it. Was it actually haunted? You bet.

Left: Riverside Hospital, 1925. *Toledo Public Library*.

Below: The hospital nursery, 1965. *Toledo Public Library*.

Opposite: Riverside Hospital wasn't all that creepy. Its pharmacy was bright and modern in the 1970s. *Toledo Blade*.

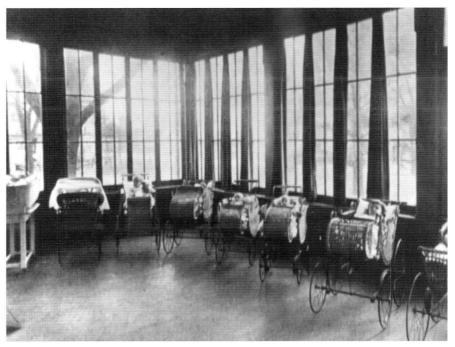

The hospital was opened in 1883 by the Sisters of Mercy. They took in young, unwed, pregnant woman and gave them a place to hide until they could deliver their baby, put it up for adaption and rejoin society without anyone knowing what happened. Back in those days, being unmarried and pregnant was heavily looked down on.

By 1945, the hospital had expanded into a fully functional hospital that also treated the sick and dying. By offering these services, the door was opened for haunted activity to move in. "My mom worked there back in the

day," said Lois Winkleman. "She would work nights and heard footsteps and doors opening and closing all the time."

In 1983, the hospital became Mercy Health. Then in 2002, it was moved to a newer building, and the old building was sold to Toledo Public Schools (TPS) for $750,000. TPS renovated half of the building for administrative offices, while the other half sat vacant and boarded up for many years until it was demolished in 2018.

While the hospital sat empty, security guards did nightly walkthroughs. They would often experience paranormal activity around the building. This included hearing unexplained noises, seeing shadow figures and hearing voices coming from the morgue area. Local ghost hunters visited the building in 2017, and at one point, they ran out of a room in terror after hearing a ghostly scream emanate from within.

CLUB BIJOU (207/209 NORTH SUPERIOR STREET)

One notorious haunted downtown location that's long gone is Club Bijou. During the 1930s, this location was a speakeasy for Chicago and Detroit mob members, and then it became the Esquire Theater in 1945. It then became a series of nightclubs starting in the 1980s: the Asylum, Clubland, Red Room, Citi Theater and lastly Club Bijou in the early 2000s.

The Asylum days are the earliest reports we have of paranormal activity occurring there. Former employee Holly Gogo remembers, "I worked at the Asylum in 1997–98. There were many instances of creepy feelings, being watched, movement out of the corner of my eye, stifled whispers and cold spots. Early one evening, I went to unlock the back door and unexpectedly lost my footing. It was as if both my feet were swept from beneath me. I went all the way down those back stairs on my butt."

The Club Bijou sign. *Toledo Public Library*.

Even after Club Bijou opened, employees and owners alike also began also experiencing activity ranging from shadow figures and unexplained voices to the pulling of their hair or clothing. The back stairwell is said to be major focal point of activity since almost everyone working there points to that area as feeling creepy. Another hot spot is located in the basement. Workers used to see two male shadow figures down there. Former employee Traeonna Wagener remembered, "A lot of people avoided the downstairs. It was a lot more aggressive feeling." She went on to explain that sometimes people were pushed or grabbed by an unseen force.

Another hot spot was located in the lobby and main office. The spirit said to be haunting this area was that of a young boy they called Billy. Wagener explained, "There was a little kid that people said died out on our sidewalk. That's the one everyone associates with pulling of the hair or moving of the keys."

The projection room was where workers often saw an apparition of a woman. They speculated that she was from the time when the building was used as a burlesque house. The projection room always gave people creepy vibes. Some people even heard ghostly voices call out to them there.

Sadly, this haunted location met its demise in 2007 to make way for the Huntington Center Sports Arena's parking lot.

Playdium (1958 Front Street)

This now vacant lot once stood from 1902 to 2012. The building started off as a bar and grill and then became a speakeasy during the 1920s Prohibition era. Secret tunnels were built underneath that connected a few of the surrounding businesses, which allowed them to smuggle alcohol around without getting caught. In 1948, the location became Playdium Lanes. Since they had a bowling alley and dance hall, it became a very popular hangout for teens throughout the '50s and '60s. The Playdium sadly went out of business during the 1980s and was sold off.

The new owner quickly began a complete remodel. Police officer Gary Bowsher stopped in and had quite the paranormal experience. "Back in the mid-'80s my partner Fred Breier and I were working midnights. We met John Kosztak, who was working on redeveloping the Playdium. Fred and I wanted to see the tunnels, so the three of us went down into the basement. There was a long hallway with an old rack of bowling balls. We walked to the end of the hallway up a bit of an incline. When we got to the end, we heard a loud thud behind us. A bowling ball had fallen off of the rack and was rolling toward us uphill! The ball continued to roll up and stopped just short of where we were standing at."

With stories like that, there's no doubting this place was haunted. Once diving into the history of this location, I found a lot of death associated with this building, starting with the death of Elizabeth Strich in 1906, John Virag in 1946, John Dudas in 1956, Charles Wasielewski in 1957 and Andrew Sarka in 1966, among others. It's a shame the Playdium is long gone, because we will never know who was haunting this area and why.

Toledo Public Library.

TOLEDO FIRE AND RESCUE STATION 13 (2154 FRONT STREET)

The abandoned fire station on Front Street was originally built in 1899. Since this station was labeled with the unlucky number 13, it's no surprise that it was taken out of service well before its time in 1936. Even after a new Station 13 was built down the street, the old location was still used as office space until 1985. During that time, employees fell victim to the ghostly echoes of the past.

Many times, they heard voices they couldn't explain, footsteps coming from empty rooms, and even horse sounds coming from the back area. Employee Peggy Fodor remembered, "If you listened real close, you could hear horses whinny from the back area from when it was used as a horse stable. I was in the building by myself one Saturday doing some paperwork, and I heard footsteps upstairs in the old quarters for the firemen."

Unfortunately, the building is all boarded up today, so investigating this location is out of the question. Since many firefighters lost their lives back then, it's highly probable that their spirits still haunt this abandoned firehouse.

TOLEDO HOSPITAL LEGACY TOWER (2142 NORTH COVE BOULEVARD)

Toledo Public Library.

This former hospital once stood from 1930 to 2016 and was replaced by a new Promedica building. Over the years, the nurses who worked there experienced all sorts of activity. According to Carolyn Mosby, "A coworker of mine who worked third shift used to tell me about sightings of a ghost dressed in period clothing wandering the hallways. She saw several different spirits roaming the hospital. They walked through walls and through closed elevator doors. She once said a family of four dressed in period clothing exited the elevator on one floor and walked right through the opposite wall. She never felt afraid of them."

It's unfortunate to hear these lost souls still roam the old hospital. I would imagine the staff at the new Promedica building also experience the same types of hauntings today.

GOODWILL (525 CHERRY STREET)

The Cherry Street Goodwill location may have closed in 2017, but previous employees still swear the place was haunted. In the 1950s, this location was known as the Old Virginia Lunch restaurant. Then in 1969, the Goodwill building replaced it.

It turns out, the Goodwill employees always felt something was off about the building, especially in the basement. Many felt like they were being watched and saw shadow figures disappear behind the numerous pillars down there. According to maintenance worker Sean Dutridge, "My office was in the basement, and I used to hear noises and see shadow figures. I was always the first person in the building to turn on all the lights. I would see stuff I can only explain as shadow figures. They were black see-through shadow-like masses. Not necessarily human-shaped, but more of a cloud. I would see it on the loading dock area and back down the hallway where my office was. I'd also hear voices,

Top: *Toledo Blade*.

Bottom: The basement of the Goodwill building is where many employees have seen shadow figures and heard strange, unexplained noises. *Toledo Blade*.

but I couldn't make out the words. They sounded off in the distance across the basement. I'd go check all the time to see who was there and couldn't find anyone."

After conducting some research on the location, I found that James Anderson died there on April 13, 1926. Could his spirit be the one haunting the building? Only a deep investigation would reveal that answer.

Mary Ann's Carry Out (8104 Dorr Street)

Mary Ann's Carry Out was demolished in the mid-2000s, but when talking to former employee Kathy Butler, it turns out this location was very haunted. "We always had things flying off the shelves and things falling for no apparent reason. Things would be in different spots in the morning from where they were left the night before. The toilet in the bathroom would also randomly flush. It was creepy, especially closing at night."

Things turned visual one evening when an apparition appeared. "Once, I was talking to someone at the counter, and in my peripheral vision, I saw a tall man wearing a red flannel shirt. I knew that the customer I was talking to was the only person in the store. So, I told them there's a man standing over there. She said, 'I see it, too.' We both turned our heads, and nobody was there."

Even the security cameras once recorded the ghostly activity. "One day, on the monitor, I saw a white fog-like figure walking around the storeroom. I called my boss, who owned the store. She came and looked at it and said, 'Oh, my God. That's my dad!'" When I reached out to the owner, she said that the incident happened back in the 1990s. During that time, the security footage was recorded over on the same VHS tape, so sadly, that footage is long gone.

18

CHALKY

The urban legend of Chalky may not have originated within the city limits of Toledo, but when this tale was posted in a Facebook group to track down its origin, a huge argument broke out over the details. After watching this heated battle unfold, I knew I had to include this legend in my book, as every teen in Toledo during the 1980s knows it. On the surface, Chalky seems to be stitched together from various rumors dating back to the 1980s, but diving behind the story spun my research in a direction that I was unprepared for.

The Chalky story goes like this: A young boy living out on a country road was playing in his yard, ran out into the street and was hit by an oncoming car. When the police arrived, they drew a chalk outline around his lifeless body. After they took the body away, the chalk outline mysteriously never faded. In the months that followed, many teenagers took notice of the chalk outline on a country road that never went away. They began gossiping about it to all their friends at school and came to the consensus that it was paranormal in nature. Shortly thereafter, the chalk outline became a tourist destination that kids, especially the teens who had just gotten their driver's licenses, had to see for themselves. This was back when *Friday the 13th* and *A Nightmare on Elm Street* became super popular, so this fit right into the same genre. It wasn't long before the legend involved having to perform a ritual that caused the spirit of the boy to produce paranormal results for visitors.

As Trisha Long recalled, "The story said if you went out there and parked on the chalk outline, turned off the car but left the lights on, something

A stock image of what Chalky appeared as.

happens. My boyfriend and his buddies did it when they were in high school. He said the car wouldn't start! Creepy!"

The Chalky legend quickly gained steam around high schools. Many kids around Toledo drove out to the site to test this for themselves. Jody Gardener remembered, "Chalky happened to us in 1989. We were from Start High School. A group of us drove out, stopped the car in front of the chalk outline, got out, jumped back in, as we were scared, and the car wouldn't start back up. After a few tries, it did! True story! That really did happen with our car!"

Sami Silver also recalled another piece of the story she heard. "I was told in the '80s there was an orphanage where the accident happened, and he wandered off the property. I drove down that road and saw the white chalk several times and had my own very strange experiences there."

Kerry Ann also visited the site with a few time-delayed results. "My friend and I went out there. We sat on top of our car, and nothing happened. We went home, and the car didn't start for three days!" So, after the car returned to normal, "he then took his brother out there, and the same thing happened!"

Everyone loved reminiscing about the Chalky story until it came time to nail down the exact location of where the chalk outline was actually located.

A huge argument ensued. Lee Soule said, "The boy who was hit by a car was out on Gunn Road by McQueen Orchards. Until they sold the property, you could still see the outline."

Nick Moose remembered differently. "You need to know your facts! It's Coder Road! Not Gunn Road. I graduated in '94 Springfield High School. The outline was on Coder Road!"

Dawn Marie Laffery chimed in, "It was Gunn Road, always and forever. I graduated '92!"

Dazz Lee Briggs added, "I remember Chalky on Gunn Road sometime between 1992 and 1995. It was hard to see at first, but once headlights hit it in the right direction, we could see it. Story I heard was that the little boy ran out after his dog and got hit by a truck."

Sarah Churchill, on the other hand, remembered the outline on Coder Road. "We rode bikes to investigate Chalky all the time. I remember Coder Road, too."

Steve Parker also added, "Not Gunn Road! It was on Coder Road, behind Sunshine Children's Home! He got out at night and was hit by car!"

Dave Sayen recalled, "The outline on Coder Road, northeast-bound before Route 20, was repainted couple times in the 1980s!"

Then you had others, like Kelly Solano, who clearly remembered Chalky being located on Gunn Road. "I remember Gunn Road and the white outline from the mid-'80s. It was a fun and scary time with friends."

The same goes for Terry Brown. "It was on Gunn Road! I live in the neighborhood!"

Melissa Jean added, "I graduated in 1992. There absolutely was a chalk outline of a boy on Gunn Road. There weren't any houses but a white one that was abandoned."

The argument ensued for weeks. There many conflicting reports from people who swore up and down that chalk outlines existed on both roads. This logically could only mean one thing: there were two separate roads where this chalk outline was found. This also meant one of them was a copycat of the other.

But this conclusion raises a few interesting questions. Which outline was the first one? Is there a real outline, or are they both fake? Did a boy even die at one of these locations or is it all just a hoax? Well, I guess we'll never be able to solve that riddle—or so I once thought.

A few weeks after the argument calmed down, Angie Schardt left a comment that changed everything about this classic urban legend. "The Chalky story is totally false! Nobody ever died on Gunn Road. That outline was made in the late '50s by my dad, Terry Seeman, my uncle and their buddies. It was the '50s, they're boys, they were bored and it was funny."

That little piece of history was pretty darn amazing. She provided names, the original location and an actual timeframe from when the Chalky prank began. Turns out, it was orchestrated by a group of school kids in the '50s. Then, at some point, the myth was revitalized in the 1980s to live on again through a whole new generation of kids.

This was a fascinating legend to piece together, but we aren't done just yet. I couldn't help but wonder if there were any more uncovered pieces of this story. While doing some massive digging on the subject, I found another piece of the puzzle that left me stunned. I ran across an article that ran in all the newspapers around the Toledo area on May 18, 1957. It reported that a murder had occurred on Gunn Road. It turns out that late one evening, thirty-year-old Charles Leichty was driving around downtown Toledo and smooth-talked fifteen year old Sonya Long into his car. She was a sophomore at Scott High School. Reports indicated that she might've been a previous babysitter for Leichty and his wife. He drove her out to the countryside, raped her and then strangled her to death. When he was done with her body, he dumped it out of his car and out onto the side of the road. That road just happened to be Gunn Road!

This blew my mind. This story filled in all the blanks I was looking for.

In the 1950s, any news of a teen abduction case would certainly have been the talk of the town, especially in public gathering spaces like churches and high schools. When Angie Schardt revealed it was her dad and his friends who drew the chalk outlines of a body on Gunn Road, they did this act around the same time that this girl was found dead alongside the same road. This leads me to wonder if the reason they started drawing chalk outlines was that the traffic on that road began to increase from so many people trying to find the exact location of the murder for themselves. This would make complete sense. What better way to show all the people driving out there where the murder site was than by drawing a physical chalk outline on the road where they

Toledo School Girl, 15, Slain; Ex-Convict Held

Chokes Scott High Student To Death

TOLEDO, O.—Charles William Leichty, 30, Lawrence avenue, is being held in Lucas county jail on a first degree murder charge in connection with the death of Sonya Sue Long, 15, Vermont avenue, Scott High school sophomore, who was found raped and murdered early Sunday beside a pond near Gunn and Salisbury roads, two miles southwest of Holland.

A news article printed on May 19, 1958. *Toledo Public Library*.

found her. So, in the end, it turns out that poor Sonya Long is our original Chalky victim.

When it comes to urban legends, little details always have a way of being twisted around as the story gets passed from person to person. This has been scientifically documented and proven in great detail. With the Chalky urban legend, we have a story from the 1950s that traversed itself through a generational gap of thirty years by word of mouth. In the 1950s, the story involved "a girl who was murdered and tossed out of a car on the side of Gunn Road." In the 1980s, the story evolved into being "a boy who was hit a car and whose body was found on the side of Gunn Road." Truly remarkable.

If you want to visit the original murder site for yourself to see if any paranormal activity occurs there, you might be out there for a while. The chalk outline has long been paved over, and no one even remembers exactly where it was.

I'm just glad I was able to finally get to the bottom of the urban legend that so many teenagers were fascinated by during the 1980s and '90s. Hopefully, Sonya Long can finally find the peace she's been looking for in the afterlife now that her full story has been revealed.

BIBLIOGRAPHY

Areis–Lucas County Auditor. https://sanborn-ohioweblibrary-org.oh0215. oplin.org/.

Blivan, Charles E. *Maumee Valley and Pioneers*. Toledo, OH, 1880.

Catholic Architecture and History of Toledo, Ohio. http://catholictoledo. blogspot.com/2007/11/mary-manse-college.html.

Charles Magus Map. Toledo, OH, 1855.

Cincinnati Commercial Tribune. "Ten Days at Toledo Park, Two of Which Entail Mysteries." August 7, 1905.

Cleveland Daily Keeper. "Sad Indeed." December 19, 1859.

Daily Ohio Statesman. "Suicide of a Well-Known Ohioan." May 19, 1865.

Dayton Times. "Two Murders During Night." April 4, 1918.

Defiance Crescent News. "Deaths." September 8, 1962.

———. "Elephant Kills His Keeper." June 15, 1914.

Delaware Gazette. Obituaries. December 30, 1859.

Delphos Daily Herald. "Toledo Player Dies from Game Injuries." November 3, 1930.

Detroit Free Press. "Committed Suicide at Toledo." March 21, 1889.

Fort Madison Evening Democrat. "Elephant Kills His Keeper." June 15, 1914.

Fremont News Messenger. "Motor Scooter Rider Killed on Road at Elmore." July 25, 1955.

———. "Murder in Toledo." August 4, 1865.

———. Obituaries. November 14, 1931.

———. Obituaries. May 19, 1956.

———. "Toledo School Girl, 15, Slain, Ex-Convict Held." May 19, 1958.

GenDisasters. "East Toledo, OH Grain Elevator Fire, Sep. 1898." http://www.gendisasters.com/ohio/17076/east-toledo-oh-grain-elevator-fire-sep-1898?page=0%2C1&fbclid=IwAR0P2sdCMxRYKDJZJzpJuqaXejRyXFF8esTMrE0rR5yaCHFiGsUZ6QBeVHQ.

Genoa Gazette. "Toledo Girl Killed in 40 Foot Plunge." June 27, 1947.

Holmes County Republican. Obituaries. December 22, 1859.

Killits, John Milton. *Toledo and Lucas County, Ohio, 1623–1923.* Vol. 1. Toledo, OH: S.J. Clarke Publishing Company, 1923.

Lake Erie Park and Casino: A Text Adventure. https://www.midstory.org/lake-erie-park-and-casino-a-text-adventure/.

Lucas County Hauntings and Legends. https://www.ohioexploration.com/paranormal/hauntings/lucascounty/.

Mansfield News Journal. "Boy 17 Loses Life on Way to Football Game." November 3, 1945.

Mary Manse College Collection. https://web.archive.org/web/20070627023423/http:/www.bgsu.edu/colleges/library/cac/ms0027.html.

Marysville Journal Tribune. Obituaries. May 28, 1934.

Mount Pleasant Daily News. "Elephant Kills His Keeper." June 15, 1914.

New Philadelphia Ohio Democrat Times. "Three People Now Drowned." July 11, 1901.

Newspaper Archive. https://newspaperarchive.com/.

Old Toledo Facebook Group. https://www.facebook.com/groups/138765346133815.

Saint Peters Cemetery. https://www.findagrave.com/cemetery/2287968/saint-peters-cemetery-(defunct).

Sanborn Insurance Maps. https://sanborn-ohioweblibrary-org.oh0215.oplin.org/.

Sandusky Register. "Incident Recalled." August 21, 1896.

———. "Toledo Girl Killed." May 9, 1947.

Sandusky Register Star News. "Blast Levels 4 Toledo Buildings." February 13, 1956.

Sandusky Star Journal. "Death of Toledo Girl Finally Solved." August 8, 1905.

———. "Zebras Attacked Park Zoo Keeper." July 18, 1929.

Telegraph Forum (Bucyrus). "Walbridge Park Zoo Leads in Equipment." March 5, 1928.

Tiffin Tribune. "Man Beaten." July 25, 1878.

Toledo Blade. "Captain Billy's Has a Healthy Plan." May 25, 1980.

————. "Carter Tops Reagan in Battle For Rally Crowds in Columbus." May 30, 1980.

————. "Corroded Gas Pipe Held as Probable Blast Cause." February 14, 1956.

————. "Does Murder Victim Haunt Trilby House?" 1990.

————. "Drowned Nun's Car Inspected." November 23, 1971.

————. "Franklin Airport Slated to Close of Sept. 15." June 26, 1952.

————. "Lasting Place in History Given Oliver House, City's First Hotel." June 1, 1971.

————. "Madison Street Cemetery." December 7, 1900.

————. "Mancy's Restaurant Destroyed by Blaze." August 14, 1973.

————. "New Holiday Inn Went Up Quickly." June 18, 1970.

————. "Professor at TU Found Dead." February 15, 1973.

————. "Toledo Getting a New Hotel." June 19, 1969.

————. "2 Killed in Crash of Plane Carrying Mail at Airport." July 8, 1971.

————. "2 TU Student Leaders Killed in Texas Car Accident." May 4, 1973.

————. "Youth's Death at Zoo Ruled Accidental." January 21, 1972.

————. "Youth's Death in Zoo Bear Cage May Have Been Suicide." January 20, 1972.

Toledo History and Nostalgia Grab Bag. https://www.facebook.com/groups/609528152413697.

Toledo Library. Polk's Toledo City Directory, 1860.

Toledo News Bee. "Cruel Car Wheels Crushed out Small Life in Instant." May 27, 1905.

————. "New $3 Million Dollar Hotel to Open Tuesday." January 17, 1927.

Toledo Obituary Search. http://obits.toledolibrary.org/obits/.

Toledo Ohio Lucas County Public Library Digital Collections. https://www.ohiomemory.org/.

Toledo Times. "Slays Brother-in-Law Who Beats Wife." April 4, 1918.

University of Toledo. "History." https://www.utoledo.edu/campus/about/history/.

YouTube. "Ghost Hunters Investigate Manos." https://www.youtube.com/watch?v=lgakXtopamk.

————. "Haunted Toledo's Legends of Ohio: Club Bijou." https://www.youtube.com/watch?v=ZpqDzdyciCo.

Zanesville Times Recorder. "Crime Experts Testify in Murder Trial."

ABOUT THE AUTHOR

C hris Bores is the star of the *Ghost Doctor* on YouTube. He is the very first ghost behaviorist who studies the behavior patterns of spirits. He has created a new approach to the paranormal field that is breaking all the rules. Bores has spent years implementing the *Tibetan Book of the Dead*, *Egyptian Book of the Dead*, psychology, sociology, quantum physics and various religions in the paranormal field to create a new approach to ghosts. These tactics have allowed him to get a ninety-minute interaction with a spirit, create a highly effective ghost classification system and pull critical information about the afterlife from the spirits themselves—he has even shown the emotional pains and the lighter side of hauntings to viewers through *Ghost Doctor*.

Chris Bores is the host of *Ghost Doctor*, the author of *Ghost Hunting 2.0*, has previously been a ghost tour guide at the Oliver House and Collingwood Arts Center in Toledo, has been featured on the Travel Channel, *Hardcore Pawn*, truTV, *Coast to Coast AM*, *Darkness Radio*, CBS News, FOX News, ABC News, *Atari: Game Over* (documentary), *Dayton Ghosts* and Star 105.5's morning radio and in the *Toledo Blade* and *Toledo Free Press*. In 2010, his channel was YouTube's fifty-fifth "Most Subscribed Channel."

If you have any stories of haunted locations Chris may have missed in Toledo, please contact him on Facebook by searching "Ghost Behaviorist Chris Bores."